An Autobiography of a Colonial Doctor

About the Author

An autobiography of a Colonial Doctor, spans the turbulent period from 1928 to 1956 and how it affected him. The doctor was born on the 1st March 1928, a leap year, on his grandfather's racecourse in Campamento, Spain missing the 29th February by a short head.

By the age of one, the family moved back to Gibraltar. His first decade of life was idyllic, for schooling was not on his calendar. At age 10 ½ years, he was sent to Hodder Place, the Jesuit preparatory school of Stonyhurst College, England, where his great uncle, father, cousin and grandson were Head of the Line- a distinction that few families achieve- worldwide. He was at Stonyhurst during the World War II years.

In 1947, he entered the gates of 'Heaven on Earth'. Trinity College, Dublin was to be his new home, and it is here that he read medicine. He graduated in arts (B.A.) in 1951 and obtained his M.B., B.C.H., B.A.O., L.A.H.I. in 1953. In 1956 he obtained his M.A. and many years later the M.I.C.G.

He met his future wife May Ringrose in 1952 and were married in 1956. They had 4 sons. After university he held several hospital appointments in England, Ireland, Scotland and Wales. He worked with the Medical Research Council in Tuberculosis when the disease was a worldwide scourge. In 1956 he returned to Gibraltar to set up practice.

He established a first class general practice. He was a Port Health Officer, and specialist to the British Military Hospital and later the Royal Naval Hospital. He was made Honorary Consultant to the Royal Navy and elected a Fellow of the Royal Society of Medicine and a numerario to the Spanish College of Otolaryngologists.

He stood for election as an Independent Nationalist Candidate. He was a prolific writer with a pro-British and an anti neo-col flavor.

An Autobiography of a Colonial Doctor

The Colonial Period

Book 1

CECIL ISOLA

authorHOUSE®

AuthorHouse™
1663 Liberty Drive
Bloomington, IN 47403
www.authorhouse.com
Phone: 1-800-839-8640

© 2011 by Cecil Isola. All rights reserved.

No part of this book may be reproduced, stored in a retrieval system, or transmitted by any means without the written permission of the author.

First published by AuthorHouse   08/09/2011

ISBN: 978-1-4567-8397-6 (sc)
ISBN: 978-1-4567-8400-3 (ebk)
ISBN: 978-1-4670-0977-5 (hc)

Printed in the United States of America

Any people depicted in stock imagery provided by Thinkstock are models, and such images are being used for illustrative purposes only.
Certain stock imagery © Thinkstock.

This book is printed on acid-free paper.

Because of the dynamic nature of the Internet, any web addresses or links contained in this book may have changed since publication and may no longer be valid. The views expressed in this work are solely those of the author and do not necessarily reflect the views of the publisher, and the publisher hereby disclaims any responsibility for them.

Contents

About the Author iii

Chapter 1   THE EARLY YEARS 1

Chapter 2   CAMPAMENTO AND GIBRALTAR 18

Chapter 3   THE SPANISH CIVIL WAR 1936 46

Chapter 4   HODDER PLACE 1938. WORLD WAR II BEGINS ... 65

Chapter 5   STONYHURST COLLEGE. LONGRIDGE. 103

Chapter 6   PEACE 120

Chapter 7   TRINITY COLLEGE, DUBLIN 1947-53 152

Chapter 8   IN ABSENTIA. 1945-56. 191

Chapter 9   HOSPITALS AND MARRIAGE 199

Chapter 10 THE RINGROSE 217

To my wonderful wife, May.

Thanks

I would like to thank my parents, now long gone, for my happiness and all too short years with them. For paying for my education at Stonyhurst and Trinity College, for without their financial help, I would not have enjoyed my years as a doctor, or met my wife. To my extended family Mema and Tuto Imossi, my aunt and uncle, who were a second mother and father, especially during the war years in Longridge, Lancashire. And to my Godmother, Aunt Kittita, who was the basis for my decision at age 9, to become a doctor. At that time she was going deaf from Otosclerosis, and for six weeks lay in bed in a darkened room, going blind. To the world Kittita was a woman, but to us she was our world. To them and to others not mentioned, a big thank you.

In the typing of this book I must thank Ms Gianella Imossi-Steele, for her typing work and encouragement in its early stages. To Ms Jane Payas, for her patience and perfection in bringing this book to fruitition. Without their help, this book would have gathered dust, for I cannot type nor am I computer literate. Most of the photographs on the book came from my records and were old when presented to Mr Miguel Peña Piña. Fortunately, he was recommended by one of my old patients. His painstaking and cheerful ways gave me the courage required to include them. To him a special thanks.

My thank you list is never ending, but I must thank Trinity College, Real Ireland Design, Dame Beulah Bewley, Dr. Margaret McMullen, Charles Culatto, and Ms Ciara Power. As for the Stonyhurst contingent, Rev Fr O´Halloran S. J, former rector, headmaster Andrew Johnson and archivist David Knight.

The list is considerable but thanks once again to all those not mentioned by name. There are however some family members that I must thank specifically. Frank Foster-Parodi, my good friend and cousin whom I met for the first time in my late sixties: the Indian connection was taken from his files. Brendan Ringrose for allowing me to read the Irish connection of the Ringrose family, able supported by Ms Nell Power, Ms May Isola, Mr Michael Ringrose, MsRita Fitzsimmons and other members of the clan. Sofie, Nicholas, Patrick, Susanna, James and Christian Isola for their encouragement and last but not least Miss Valerie Ringrose-Fitzsimmons, a journalist with Telefis-Eirann, for editing my book. By the time, Valerie finished the correction, with many red ink lines, reminded me of my first two weeks at Hodder Place, the preparatory school of Stonyhurst. I was aged ten, last in class and it's eldest.

Chapter 1

THE EARLY YEARS

Birth on the Racecourse

Not many babies are born in the centre of a racecourse, and fewer of them miss the 29th of February as their birth date, by a short head. I was born on the first of March 1928 at the Parodi (my great uncle's) house on Matias Murto's (my maternal grandfather), racecourse at Campamento, Spain. The decision for this venue was based on political, residency and obstetric reasons. The hospital service in the adjoining town of La Liñea was non-existent, and the risks of Puerperal Sepsis and death at the Colonial Hospital, Gibraltar, were substantial. The political decision as to whether I was born British and Gibraltarian had already been legislated a few years earlier at my father's insistence, so my birth in Spain was of no nationality consequence. As my parents were British and Gibraltarian by birth, my nationality and status would follow theirs, if I were registered at the La Linea's British consulate. I was. With little or no antenatal care available locally, 'Villa de la Concepcíon' was a superb choice for my delivery. This despite the fact that the house was surrounded by many racehorses and with the possible deadly side effects, that an untreatable tetanus would entail.

The Colonials and Stonyhurst

In the latter part of the nineteenth century, a visiting Jesuit came to Gibraltar, seeking 'the right' Gibraltarians for a good Catholic education at Stonyhurst College, England. Needless to say, the selected students had to have the financial backing that such a fine English education would entail, as well as the necessary intelligence to succeed at the College. Three such men were my grandmother's brothers Horace, Ernest and Augusto Parodi. They were all accepted to Stonyhurst. Horace later had the distinction of being Head of the Line 1886-1887; a distinction held by my late father, Albert Isola 1917-1918; my late cousin Charles Isola 1958-1959; and by my grandson Nicholas Isola 2008-2009. The foundation for a par-excellence English Jesuit education was a blessing in disguise for the Gibraltarians. It gave those who went to the UK, the same confidence and privilege that those who came from the UK had when in colonial Gibraltar. Better still, their Jesuit education was acceptable, not only to the military, but to the colonial establishment as well. The Jesuits knew all about the colonial 'odd practices' and guaranteed that the Parodi brothers were versed to counter any perceived colonial injustices, should they have shown their ugly faces. Gibraltar, though a Crown Colony, was in effect a fortress and as such, military law was paramount: fair but firm.

Members of the Parodi-Isola family were the first Gibraltarians to receive a public school education at Stonyhurst and for nearly 130 years since then, have maintained an unbroken attendance. The youngest Isola recruit is my grandson Christian who entered Stonyhurst in 2008 with a scholarship. Previous to that he was at Beaumont. His older brother Nickie left Stonyhurst in 2009 after a very successful school career. His last three prizes were won at Rhetoric, the school's highest class. There he won the Chemistry prize twice; the Award for Leadership and was a joint winner of the Rugby Cup for his outstanding contribution to the sport. He also completed the London Marathon at a good pace in less than 4 hours, at just 18 years old.

In the late nineteenth century the British Empire had the largest merchant marine in the world. In Gibraltar it was fairly obvious, for ninety per cent flew the red duster. Liners called here daily and the port offered worldwide shipping connections. Whilst liners anchored daily in the Bay of Gibraltar, the travel time of over six days from Gibraltar to the UK restricted the Parodi boys to summer holidays only. It was a heavy but acceptable price to pay, if the benefits of an excellent Catholic education were included in its summation.

The Empire Builders

With a successful education at Stonyhurst, the doors were fully opened for the Parodis should they have wished to serve the British Empire. The three proceeded to Oxford University. Tragically the second eldest, Augustus died from Typhoid fever whilst on holiday in Campamento. Following graduation, Horace returned to Gibraltar and married the beautiful Elena Haynes. He had a successful legal practice (B1). Blessed by three daughters, and in keeping with our Genoese roots, the young girls were sent to Rome for a convent education. The waters between Gibraltar, Genoa and Naples were very well served by the Italia Lines. They traversed the seas between Italy, and the United States and Italy and the Argentine: Gibraltar being its first and last port to and from the Americas.

Gibraltar, in the first quarter of the 20th Century, was not only a fortress and a social hub, but also an important staging post for world travel. Liners calling here daily served India, Australia, New Zealand, Singapore, Hong Kong, the East Asian Dutch Possessions, South Africa and all Africa, North and South America, Western Europe, and a host of other places. Social events were common, and racing at Campamento and Gibraltar was held on a regular basis. The Calpe Hunt was also in full swing and the Spanish authorities were accommodating to our Governor. The Empire reigned supreme and Gibraltar was the social nexus for southern Spain.

CAMPAMENTO RACECOURSE, SPAIN. A.

Race Cup and inscription.

Regalo de S.M. el Rey Don Alfonso XIII a la Sociedad de Carreras de Caballos de Andalucia.
REunion de Mayo 1905, ganada por Don. I. Cazes y Ms. Murto con el caballo "Lutteur", montado por el jockey M. Goodman.

There is a small gold plate mounted on the base, which reads:
Presento la parte que me corresponde de esta copa a mi amigo L. Cazes en el dia de su casamiento. Matias Murto 23/05/1906

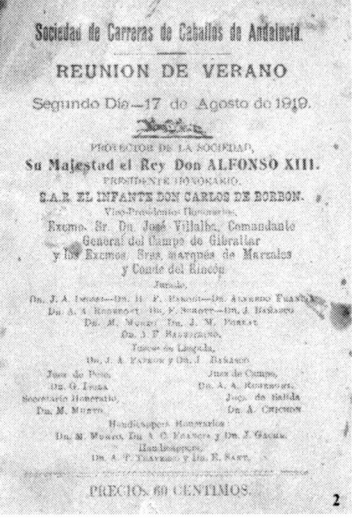

Racecard.

In the first race of this meeting, number 1, was called Ghadir and was owned by Lt. Higgins. His racing colours were "la bandera irlandesa" (the Irish flag). His other horse for that meeting was "Somme". The Easter Rising in Ireland was in 1916 and many thousands of Irish died in the battle of the Somme (1916)

Magda - Ultor - Sol y Sombra - Selis on morning exercises. Playa Poniente *(1921)*

As seen from the Grandstand.

Entering the Racecourse.

A.

Kitty Murto behind the Grandstand.

Kitty Murto outside her home in "Villa Ena", Avenida España. *(1923)*.

Stonyhurst College *(1917)*. Albert Isola 4th left, standing.

The Murto Family *(1916)*.

Verdun, France *(1919)*.
Adelaide and Mema Murto.

A.

Tennis Champions. Juanita's husband was Colonel Franco's senior in the Barracks.
Juanita 2nd left.

On honeymoon. Nice, Southern France.
Albert and Lali Isola.

The wedding of Albert Isola and Adelaide Murto at Villa de la Concepcion, Campamento.

The Colonials Abroad

Ernest

Ernest Parodi, my great uncle (K8), I knew throughout my early life. After joining the colonial legal service, he rose to an Appeal Court Judge in a British African colony. He married Cleo Peacock late in life, and they had no children, probably as a result. The Peacocks were a well-known shipping agency in Gibraltar and on John Peacock's death, in keeping with English colonial tradition, his widow and 2 daughters returned to England. His managing clerk, the late John Mackintosh, Gibraltar's greatest benefactor, became its new owner. Whilst Great Uncle Ernest had all the characteristics of a successful judge, his wife lacked one important criterion. It appeared she had no idea of time. Punctuality at any governmental function is the most important of colonial social rules. For an Appeal Court judge to be late at Government House did not merit a recommendation and within a year or two, Great Uncle Ernest had resigned and was back in London in legal practice. Cleo's other sister, Carlota, had produced two extraordinary children; Verona, one of the 10 most beautiful women I was ever to see, and Gerry who oozed with personality, and was a handsome and attractive man about town. Verona married a Scott in name (and nationality) and endearingly called by all, Scottie. Gerry married the Hon. Mrs Hannah Marks.

Horace (B1)

With a Roman education, good looks, manners and being bilingual, Horace's daughters, Olga, Muriel (later called Carmen)

3 Secretary's Lane,
Gibraltar.
23rd May '12.

Dear Mary,

Many thanks for your lovely letter, with your kind and flattering words. Cecil was delighted you enjoyed the book; he's put a few years into it, I can assure you.

Your Easter card was much appreciated — thanks. I have been in & out of hospital over the last few months — following a strangulated hernia, operation plus a few complications following it. Thank God I am now recovering and feeling better by the day. Cecil is keeping well for 84 yrs. D.g. and we live quite a simple life.

The family members are well, both generations.

Keep in touch, and above all, keep well,

Cecil joins me in sending you fondest love,
May

and Berenice, were unlikely to remain unmarried for long. Somewhere along the line, they were bound to meet their life-long partners. Berenice (B8), the youngest, married Burr Eastwood, Uncle to Clint Eastwood, one of Hollywood's most famous actors; that marriage ended in divorce plus one daughter: Ines. Olga married USN Captain Dyer, and one of their children, Elenita (B9) married a US military man, Jim Batte who later became Brigadier-General and was Chief-of-Staff, at the White House, Washington.

The Parodis in India

In 1922, my Great-Uncle Horace died. (Stonyhust obituary B1). After his death, his wife Elena (B5), daughters Muriel (B7) and Berenice (B8) migrated to the United States. The other daughter Olga was already married and had left Gibraltar. It is with Elena and Carmen (Muriel) that the Indian colonial connection unfolds. Whilst Elena was in the United States, a very good friend of the family of several years standing proposed marriage. He now lived in India. She accepted. His name was Dr Martin Onslow Forster, later Sir. He was the Director of the Indian Institute of Science, its longest serving director, having been in the post for eleven years. He was the last European to hold this post. He had all the qualifications that a distinguished scientist can have: a Fellow of the Royal Society, a PhD from Würzburg, Germany and so forth: too numerous to mention. The 'Who's Who' of 1928 was good evidence of a man with a brilliant brain. Their marriage could be described as one made in heaven.

Though unmarried on her arrival in India, Carmen was later to meet her partner-for-life: Donald Moyle Field, later Sir. He had come to India as a serving military officer and was gazetted to the Indian Army. Within 8 years of service, he had been transferred to the Foreign and Political Department, and one of his first duties, was to be placed in the staff of the late Amir Habibulla of Afghanistan on his official visit to India. He held various appointments in India, and just to name a few: he was British Joint Commissioner at Leh; held the under-secretarships of his department in the southern states of Rajputana, Chamba (Punjab States), Jaipur and the southern states of Central India and Malwa. He retired in 1935, when he was awarded a CIE.

He then accepted a pressing invitation from Maharaja Sir Umaid Singh Bahadur to become his Chief Minister in Jodhpur, which he held for 11 years.

Shortly before the Second World War, in 1938, Donald married Carmen (Muriel) Parodi, in Mysore and returned to Jodhpur for duty. As a wedding present the Maharaja gave them a Wacko aeroplane, with which they learnt to fly and which they sold at the outbreak of the Second World War. The plane later crashed in Delhi, killing all four people.

Carmen became a very popular first lady in support of Donald. She was kind hearted; beautiful; an accomplished speaker, and fluent in four languages. She was intelligent, vivacious and the perfect hostess. When pregnant the Maharaja ordered that a broad-gauge saloon, for her personal use, be attached to her train from Bombay to Bangalore, where she would give birth to her only child.

As a result of their valued positions and with two first ladies worthy of their salt, the Forsters and Fields were in for years of entertaining and being entertained and at the highest level. Amongst the many Maharajas, Maharanis, Princes of Indian origin, they met the ex-King of Greece (B6). Alfonso XIII of Spain (B11-15); the Nizam of Hyderabad; the polo playing prince: the Maharaja of Jaipur; Admiral the Lord Louis Mountbatten (B16); Jawaharlal Nehru and so on.

Pandit Nehru was smitten by Carmen and a letter by him written at Ormond House, St James' Street, London SW1 dated 3 July 1938 I quote verbatim:

> *Dear Señorita*
>
> *I want to keep my promise and send you my book. But before I do so I should like to be sure of your address. Could you kindly let me know where I am to send it?*
>
> *Yours sincerely*
> *JAWAHARLAL NEHRU*

It is to be noted that Nehru, had an eye for the ladies and Carmen was very pretty in those days. This was one way to find her address.

In 1933, Martin Forster retired. The Maharaja of Mysore gave the family a 100-year lease on an old property known as Old Banni Mantap (OBM) situated about 2 miles from Mysore City. Elena and Carmen set about turning OBM (B5) into a delightful home in Andalusian style, which was much admired by all who visited.

Just after they started to transform the house, His Highness the Maharaja had invited the exiled King Alfonso XIII (B11-15) with his son Don Juan de Bourbon and the Duke of Miranda for a visit to Mysore. H.H. realised what a help Elena and Carmen would be, as they spoke fluent Spanish. They were both invited by HH to the

Lalitha Mahaj Palace (B14) in Mysore where King Alfonso and Don Juan were entertained. The Maharaja's brother, H.H. the Yuvaranja (B14), presided over the occasion and Mrs Forster (Elena) sat next to him and opposite the King.

King Alfonso expressed his interest in the project at OBM, so Elena offered to show him the house and he cordially accepted the invitation. It was a delightfully informal visit and they seemed to enjoy the relaxed atmosphere there, no doubt enlivened by the customary tray of assorted drinks!

There is no evidence either verbally, by correspondence or notes, on the subject of Gibraltar having been discussed at OBM, but there is a 100 per cent certainty that it was. As Elena was not of Indian origin and looked more Mediterranean than Scandinavian, Alfonso XIII would have asked her; 'Where were you born?' From there the conversation would have turned to Gibraltar and Genoa.

King Alfonso XIII of Spain (B11)

King Alfonso XIII was always desirous of maintaining the friendliest relations between his country and Britain. Good Anglo-Spanish relations then existed, so when King Edward VII (B10) visited Gibraltar in 1903, it did not provoke protests in Spain, as was to be the case when Queen Elizabeth II visited Gibraltar in 1954. King Alfonso's plan for Gibraltar was a 99-year lease, rather than one in perpetuity, a rental of £1 per annum, which he would collect personally on a yearly basis from the Governor. On that day both flags would be flown on the Rock. He put his idea to King George V on more than one occasion. How much of this was known to my grandfather, Matias Murto, or to the Parodis in India is difficult to discern, for there is no verbal or written evidence to that effect.

In 1917, when the killing fields of France were digesting at a rapid rate the armies of Britain and France, Lloyd George, Prime Minister of Great Britain, bethought that if he could induce Spain to join the Allies, the Spanish troops could be brought to the Western Front... A memorandum was drawn up on the advisability of exchanging Gibraltar for Ceuta and a number of officers were trained to act as Liaison officers for the Spanish Army.

In that same year, King Alfonso XIII again made his previous proposal of a 99-year lease to King George V personally. It should be noted that King Alfonso XIII was married to Princess Victoria Eugene, a direct descendant of Queen Victoria of England.

Frank Parodi Forster

Frank Parodi Forster (B5, K10), like myself, had three mothers and two fathers, for that is what the Forsters and Fields were to him. He was probably, one of the last men to understand and see for himself, the last days of Imperial Britain in India. He integrated fully into the system and as a result benefited from his behaviour.

He wrote:

> *As a small boy I was aware of the stunning beauty of some Princesses and would enjoy talking to them. I loved being taken for motor-car rides, for the cars that the Princes owned, were the best of the world: Deusenberg, Delage, Hispano-Suisa, Rolls Royce, Bentley and Minerva. The two outings which were the most memorable being the Deusenberg driven by the Nizam of Hyderbad's second son who was a very friendly*

and handsome Prince. He was married to my favourite Princess Nilofer, who incidentally gave me a delightful present, namely a snow white pony called Snowball, who arrived fully saddled and bridled in brand new leather. What a wonderful surprise!

The second outing was in a new Bentley driven by the legendary polo playing Prince, the Maharaja of Jaipur. That drive took place in Ootacamund (Ooty) in the Nilghiri Hills during the annual gathering of Princes and various popular social gathering where eveyone of any importance wanted to be seen.

Frank was sent to Oundle School, England and in the summer of 1940, joined the Royal Air Force. By November 1941, he was flying Spitfires, and by February 1942, he was on his way to the Far East war zone. On his return to the United Kingdom, he met Eileen Checkley (K10). It was love at first sight and within 4 months, they were married.

In their twilight years, they settled in Southern Spain, with a good view of The Rock. The rest of Frank's family and grandchildren settled in North America.

STONYHURST MAGAZINE. B.

In Memoriam.

HORACE P. PARODI (O.S. 1881).

With deep regret we announced the death of Horace Parodi in the last number of the *Magazine*.

Horace Parodi, son of the late Richard E. Parodi, of Gibraltar, came to Stonyhurst on September 30th, 1881, and spent seven years here, leaving from Philosophy in 1888. Whilst at school he was a most prominent boy, to the fore in work and games. His class, a large one, —it numbered 37 in Rudiments—was rather a famous one, and it was fortunate in its Masters, having Father James Robinson, in Rudiments and Grammar, Father H. Walmesley, in Syntax and Poetry, and Father Cyprian Splaine, in Rhetoric. Among Parodi's classmates were the present Archbishop of Bombay, Major Trappes-Lomax, Christopher Stapleton, Francis Synnott, Edward Blount, Father F. Ratcliffe, Charles Mathew, Alan Stern, Father Cuthbert Cary-Elwes, to mention but a few names. In competition with these and others Parodi more than held his own. Medals and prizes he collected with gratifying regularity, carrying off in his last two years as a boy the Lomax prize, the Kelly Latin Verse, and the O'Gorman Latin Prose Prizes. In 1888 he matriculated. In 1886—'7 he was Prefect of the Sodality and Head of the Line, posts in which he was held in great respect as a boy of conscientious and sincere character.

The *Magazines* of the 'eighties bear testimony to Horace Parodi's successful activities in the Stonyhurst Debating Society, then under the direction of its founder, Father John Gerard. He is remembered as an admirable debater, and he secured an early experience in the art of public speaking which served him well in after life.

Philosophers in 1888. He was a very good runner, and the 100 yards race in the Athletic Sports, run on Whit-Tuesday, 1888, is still remembered, A. de Mun being first, Horace Parodi second, and his brother, E. Parodi, third.

Three years after leaving Stonyhurst Horace Parodi was called to the Bar, June 10th, 1891. He began to practise in Gibraltar in the following year. He soon attained to a large practice. In

He was keenly interested in sport, being for some time President of the Mediterranean Rowing Club, and one of the founders of the Andalusian Racing Club.

Hotel Principe Alfonso, Campamento.

The following account of the funeral is from the *Gibraltar Chronicle* :—

The funeral of the late Mr. Horace P. Parodi, which took place yesterday afternoon, was attended by a large number of friends and sympathizers, the Right Rev. H. G. Thompson, O.S.B., Roman Catholic Bishop of Gibraltar, officiating at the Cathedral of St. Mary the Crowned, and the chief mourners being Mr. Richard Parodi, Mr. Albert Parodi (brothers), and Mr. Albert Isola (nephew of the deceased). Lieut. Chaworth-Musters, A.D.C., represented His Excellency the Governor, and among those present were Vice-Admiral Long, U.S. Navy, His Honour the Chief Justice, the Hon. Colonial Secretary, the Hon. Attorney-General, the Hon. Colonial Treasurer, the Hon. Mr. A. Mosley, the Hon. Mr. J. Andrews-Speed, the Hon. Mr. A. C. Carrara, Mr. J. R. Crook, Mr. Rowan-Hamilton, Mr. J. Discombe, Mr. J. Cochrane, Mr. E. P. Griffin, Mr. H. J. King, Dr. Lyons, Mr. J. Porral, Mr. A. Galliano, Mr. R. Sprague, Mr. G. Gaggero, Major Cooper, representatives of the clergy, the legal and medical professions, the Consular Body, the press, the mercantile community, the Little Sisters of the Poor, the Sisters of Bon Secours, the orphans of the Asylum of St. John of God, etc., etc. There were a large number of beautiful floral offerings. The business houses closed their premises as the funeral procession traversed Main Street on the way to the North Front Cemetery, where the interment took place.

I was always struck by the great forbearance he showed throughout his illness, that lasted some ten to fifteen years.

An abridged version of a very long obituary.

THE PARODIS IN INDIA.   B.

Carmen Parodi (Lady Field), Frank Forster and Elena Parodi (Lady Forster).

Parodi Crest.

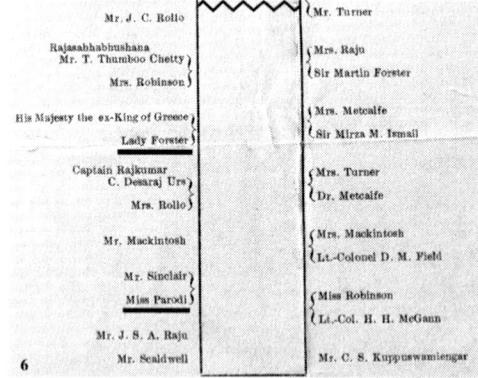

Carmen Parodi.

Berenice.

Elenita portrait.

THE PARODIS IN INDIA.   B.

King Alfonso XIII.

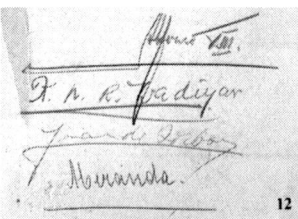

Signatures.

King Edward VII on His official visit to Gibraltar *(1903)*.

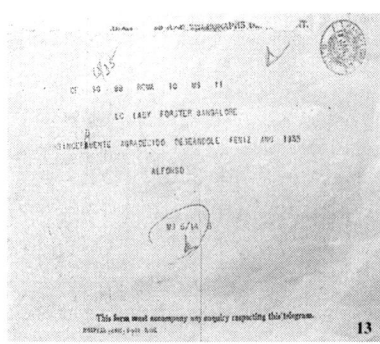

Telegram.

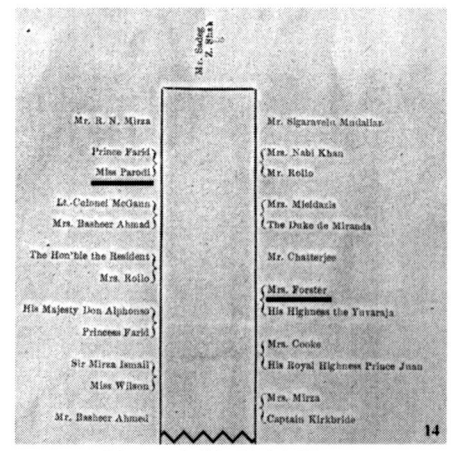

Dinner at Lalitha Mahaj, Mysore *(1st March 1933)*.

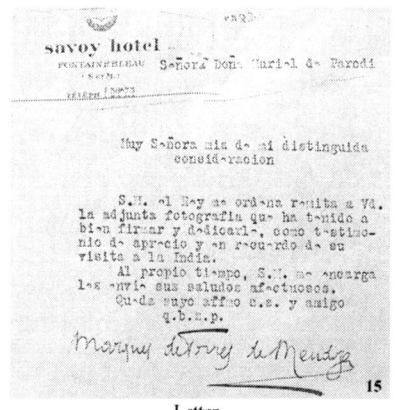

Letter.

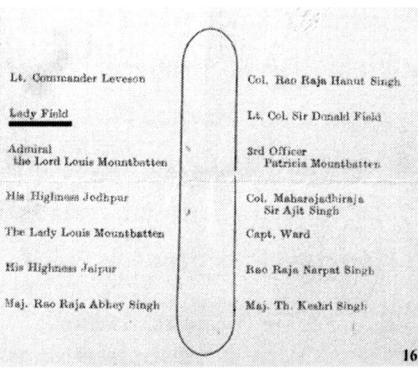

H.H. Jodhpur *(1945)*.

Chapter 2

CAMPAMENTO AND GIBRALTAR

Three Mothers Two Fathers

Matias Murto (A9) was my maternal grandfather. His wife, Magdalena Bellamy, died 18 months before I was born from liver cancer at the early age of 52 years. My grandfather was reputed to be one of the richest and most generous benefactors of the area. He owned Campamento Racecourse (A4, A5), many racehorses, adjoining lands, properties and other thriving businesses. With my great uncle Horace Parodi and a few others (A2), he founded 'La Sociedad de Carreras de Caballos de Andalusía', of whom El 'Protector de La Societad' was Su Majesta el Rey Don Alfonso XIII. Its Honorary President was S.A.R. El Infante Don Carlos de Borbon (A1, A2). Unfortunately for him, and more so for his family, he was born with a compulsive gambling gene. A casino built at the southern end of Campamento, 'El Principe Alfonso' (B 2) was to be his downfall. Bankrupt by gambling debts, he sailed one night to the New World and settled in Asuncíon, Paraguay a year or so before my birth. With his entrepreneurial nature, it was not long before he grasped the financial benefits of cotton exportation to the Lancashire mills of Great Britain. He did very well, but with the end to British India, his business went partially south. He remarried, had a new family and forgot his duties to his old family and financial guarantors. They had helped him to find his new world; a world that would have been impossible, without the emotional and financial support of his family and friends, who acted in unison and with a Christian fervour.

Matias' disappearance and the loss of Magdalena left a huge void in their lives. My mother, her two sisters, Kittita and Mema and Mema's boyfriend Tuto Imossi filled up this loss in no uncertain way. Within a year of my birth, we had moved to our new home at 3 Secretary's Lane; my parents, my brother Willie, sister Lennie and aunts Kittita and Mema. I therefore was blessed with three exceptional mothers and two fathers, for that was what Tuto became to me. My younger brother Peter was born in Gibraltar a year later.

Kittita's influence and her illnesses were to be the main reason for my eventually deciding to read medicine. My interest began at the age of nine and by twelve, I was determined to be a doctor. How, never entered my mind, because I was intellectually very lazy.

3 Secretary's Lane (D2, D3, D6, D13)

Our colonial house adjoined the Brigadier's house and his stables. On our southern side lay the senior military officers' stables, with their homes opposite ours. Sticky flypaper ensured the death of hundreds of horse flies daily. Yet despite this scourge, I cannot recall a case of food poisoning ever occurring at home; such were our staff's good practices. The side effects of our equine neighbours were also put to good use. Their nitrogenous waste made our garden the best in town. My mother won most of the major prizes at the flower shows.

There was no electricity upon our arrival at Secretary's Lane (D3) but when it finally came it was a blessing. However, earthing had not yet made its scientific mark locally and within two years of being centrally connected, Willie became sealed to the wall light socket. My mother in her attempt to save him was equally frozen in place. Had it not been for Kittita's quick thinking, in switching off the mains, a major tragedy would most certainly have occurred. Proper earthing in the house was a post World War II development.

We had no freshwater other than the rainwater contained in our below ground reservoir and our fresh drinking water was brought in by donkey in large caskets from San Roque (D 7). This was safe to drink, whereas the water in our cistern was not. There were no water heaters available in town and subsequently buckets of hot water were brought up to the first floor for our nightly baths from the kitchen's large coal-fired cooker. It was to be another five years before gas was available. Hot water now flowed in the bathroom at the turn of a knob—a great technical advance.

The fridge came years later, and with it real progress. Before refrigeration, large slabs of ice were all that was available to keep fresh food from rotting. There was no fresh milk available in Gibraltar and Spanish milk might have contained the Tubercle bacillus, an excellent reason to avoid it. However the Governor had one cow for his own personal needs. She grazed at Governor's

Meadow, a luscious grassy field specifically reserved for all her needs. For the rest of the population it was Nestlé's Ideal Milk, though some preferred the powder forms. I never saw a cow until my arrival at Hodder in 1938, when I learnt to distinguish the cows from the bulls! I had great respect for all UK cows since my only practical knowledge of the animal was the bull, as seen in bullfight posters.

The Settled

Lucilla Parodi (N1) was my paternal grandmother. She had five brothers: three of whom went to Stonyhurst and Oxford and two remained here. William Isola married Lucilla on 3 April 1897 and their first child Lourdes was born on 17 February the following year. By coincidence and unknown to us until later, I married May 59 years later on the same day and month and our first son Brian was born on 17 February, also in the following year. Lucilla was not a great socialite, for I rarely saw her outside her house, and when seen, she was either on her way to the Cathedral or on her way back. She was a devout Catholic.

Our Sunday lunches were always held at my paternal grandparents' house. With the help of their daughter Maruja and cook Carmen, lunch was invariably of 5-Star standards. We were usually seventeen at table, and after the war, the number increased to nineteen, as the result of cousins Charlie and Francis joining the family fold. To feed 19 on a regular bi-monthly basis, kept aunt Maruja and Carmen fully occupied. Sleeping at night was difficult due to the rowdiness of the Royal Navy, when alcoholically oiled. My grandparents' house was run along Victorian lines: punctuality;

good manners; respect for the ladies, and no smoking in front of them, or in the dining room.

My grandfather or Papa Willie (N1), as we all called him, was quite the opposite of Lucilla. He loved the fresh air, and it was unusual to see him at their home—106 Main Street except at meal times. He was a man oozing with charm, who loved his cigars, and was rarely seen without one. To walk with him down Main Street required considerable patience, since 15 metres was the most one could walk, without being stopped by one of his innumerable friends. He was President of the Casino Calpe for many years, and Company Secretary to Smith Imossi. Every night, without exception, he would visit us for two hours at bath time, until we left for schooling in England. He had two sisters and one brother Arturo. Arturo and his wife Mariquita had five daughters and one son Lolo. The five daughters were exceptionally beautiful and full of fun. As a result, the five most eligible Gibraltarian men surrendered to their charms, and all made good wives. Two married the Lavarello brothers. The other three married Carrara, Rugeroni and Thompson. The good looks gene has remained in their families to this day. Add charm and all is well if marriage is the first or final option. It usually is! Lolo married one of the Smith sisters.

I was never interested in my genealogy and to go to the Cathedral to look it up, I considered a waste of time. From 1938 to 1956, other than for holidays, I was either in the UK or Eire, and when I returned in 1956, I was too busy to investigate it. Much of my genealogy was relayed to me through word of mouth, mainly from my mother's side, even though occasionally my Great Uncle Horace's legal documents' wax stamp brought others into the fold. One such was

Tony Lombard, a Gibraltarian intellectual and lawyer. He wrote to Genoa on the Coat of Arms of the Parodi family:

"As I mentioned to you, because the wax seal cemented together the green ribbons which bound the pages of the Will, I assumed that the Coat of Arms impressed upon the wax belonged to the Testator. The Director of the Italian Heraldic College informed me that the Coat of Arms belonged to the . . . . 'very ancient and Noble Parodi House, the best known in Genoa and all over the region of Liguria . . . . ' Your Great Uncle Horace Parodi acted for the Testator and he must have sealed the binding on the pages by impressing his family's Coat of Arms on the wax seal (B4). You will note from the Count's headed paper that he is the editor of the Golden Book of the Italian Nobility and as a member of the Parodi family you may be entitled to being registered in the book." I did not follow it up, but I knew if I wished to pursue this side of the family it could be traced to the year 504 A.D. But it was in the Murto's genealogy that I found some interesting throwbacks, for they were born outside Gibraltar. My maternal grandmother was of Irish extraction (Bellamy) as was my great grandmother, whose name could not be more Irish than it was: Mary Murphy. This side of my family had migrated from the west of Ireland and had settled in Spain.

EARLY YEARS.

C.

Annual Fancy Dress Party. *(1931)*

Campamento beach. Brothers and sister. *(1929)*

Montagu Bathing Pavillion. Cecil, Johnnie Stagnetto and Peter. *(1934)*

Haile Selassie. Emperor of Abyssinia, with Detective-Inspector Gilbert leaving. Government House. *(1935)*

Cecil at Vichy, France. *(1932)*

THE CIVIL WAR. SPAIN VERBOTEN.   D.
ITS LOCAL EFFECTS.

A Gibraltar free of cars; stables within the fortress walls; an idyllic centre for recreation and roaming; horse racing; picnics at North Front; beautiful gardens; fish galore in the bay; streets that were washed thrice a day and were spotless; clean beaches; that was the Gibraltar of the Civil War era.

Ernest Britto.
My educational saviour.
(1936-38).

Charlie Stagnetto and
Hector Capurro.

Secretarys Lane.
(No cars).

Willie Isola. Ragged
Staff, now Queensway.
(No cars).

Calentita; a delicious pasta.
Genoese in origin. *J. Morello.*

Paddy Imossi. Officers' stables in
Secretary Lane.

Water carrier. *C. Culatto.*

Angel Rugeroni with the girls on a fishing trip. *(1938).*

D.

Three smart girls "to be": growing up.

Building Aerodrome *(1939)*.

The programme.

The **"Rose and the Ring"** play held at the Methodist building. *(April 1940)*.
Sixteen years to the day, I married the Ring and the Rose: Ringrose.

Paddy and Kittita. "To the world Kittita was our aunt. To us she was our world".

The Frontier. *(1937)*.
"The gates to hell".

Kittita, though plagued with increasing deafness due to Oto-sclerosis, was not only a fine sportswoman but a bluestocking as well. By the age of thirteen, she had written articles that were published not only in Gibraltar, but in Spanish newspapers as well. She was an accomplished writer. Had she lived in England, she would certainly have joined the suffragettes, for she believed sincerely in women's rights, which in this area were non-existent.

She was a superb tennis player (A11) and won many singles and doubles events in Andalucía. Her lady partner for these events was her cousin, Juanita (A11). She married a Spanish military man, who reached the status of colonel before he was medically discharged with Pulmonary Tuberculosis. His junior at the barracks was Colonel Franco (later General). I met her on several occasions after the war, when we visited her in Seville. What a lovely person she was! Her widow's pension was totally inadequate, as was the case for most pensioners throughout Spain. Kittita was not only a horse owner but an accomplished rider as well. Had it not been for her sex, she would have jockeyed, many of her racehorses passed the winning post (A6, A7).

Of my four grand parental names, only 1 survived: Isola. By the late seventies, the names Parodi, Murto and Bellamy had locally become extinct, due to the predominance of females in those lines. The male Isolas multiplied. Our Murto family tree still survives in Paraguay and Spain, but Parodi and Bellamy are gone forever.

Albert R Isola (O13, O14)

My father, like his uncles before, was accepted by Stonyhurst, shortly after the outbreak of World War I. He was fourteen years old. He was known to be clever enough to be placed in Poetry, the second highest class at Stonyhurst. He was in that class for 1 year. The following three years were spent in Rhetoric—its highest class. Due to submarine warfare, he did not return to Gibraltar. He attained 'all that was possible at school, and before he left Stonyhurst in July 1918 had started to read law, and in 1920 he passed his finals and was called to the Gibraltar Bar. As a lawyer he was very successful. He had a clear, logical mind, was an excellent speaker and won many well-deserved triumphs. The Gibraltar Chronicle's obituary described him as a 'brilliant advocate and past master in the art of cross-examination' and the judge in court on the day of his funeral said: "He commanded the respect which is due to a barrister of integrity, of a high degree of skill and of unlimited industry on his clients' behalf." He was a member of the Executive Council and was the first and only member to be elected to the First Legislative Council at the first count. He was a K.C. and J.P. He was President of the Gibraltar Jockey Club, Life President of the Mediterranean Racing Club and President of the Casino Calpe for many years. He was on innumerable boards and committees. His services to Gibraltar were invaluable, before, during and after the war. He was quite prepared to stand politically alone. He remained independent in mind and politics and believed strongly in the politics of consensus, so important for the small Colony of Gibraltar, where divisive politics would, with time, show their ugly face. He was against the colonial concept of 'Divide and Rule', for you cannot serve the best interests of the people in a divided community and assembly. At Stonyhurst he was Head of the Line, Prefect of the Sodality, Captain of the Football XI and a host of other appointments.

He was, as the Chronicle wrote in his obituary "A fearless advocate of the causes in which he believed (O13, O14). Mr Isola was in his hey-day, as brilliant with his pen as he was with his speeches. "There will be many who remember the sting in his articles signed 'Beccles' (L1-5) in El Annunciador in pre war days. "Of his forensic ability, it used to be said 'if your case is weak in law consult Mr Isola . . . ."

My father on a point of principle did not apply for membership of the Garrison Library, despite the fact that he was a K.C. and would have been accepted. The Garrison Library was closed to natives and as such, only a handful applied and were accepted. My father did not wish to pursue such a 'Privilege'.

His clients were not only Gibraltarians but Spaniards, mainly from Barcelona, Madrid, Seville and Malaga. On the 19 January 1930, he was awarded the (Spanish) Peace Medal: la Medalla de la Paz de Marruecos (O 10). He wore this medal with the Coronation Medal (O8) for the photograph of the Queen's visit (R 1). He had no other medals or decorations bestowed upon him by the Colonial Government, for you cannot serve two masters: the people and the Colonial Government. He preferred the former. He was the first Gibraltarian to take up the Gibraltar cause. In the First Legislative Council, he was the only candidate to be elected on the first count (O1): such was his popularity.

In the court-room he demanded respect and when two battle cruisers 'collided' in the 'Strait', the ships' captains were summoned to the Admiralty Court. He reminded one naval captain who was in command in the court-room. After the case, he was carried shoulder high to the court gates. The court room was always packed whenever Albert Isola appeared. In one of the

Civil War cases, the S.S. Stancroft (G) the British National Press descended on Gibraltar, for two of Britain's most famous legal brains DN Pritt KC, MP and Geoffrey Bing, were to appear for the defence. Publicity for the case had a world-wide audience, for it was a left-right civil war case.

In 1940, we crossed Spain on our way to school in England. My father had a special pass to allow us through war-torn Spain. The pass was issued by the highest authority in Madrid. It was questioned at Irun's border and my father had to wait there until it was cleared by the Madrid authorities.

He was a DIN (Do It Now) man and would always discourage us, if we pursued the DIM (Do it Mañana) way. Shortly after World War II, he wanted to settle Gibraltar's legal status and establish our rights, which were not covered by other treaties. Our status was high on his agenda. As a KC he was very confident that we cold win, but unfortunately, the other elected politicians, whose knowledge and experience on this matter, appeared to be well below the norm, disagreed with him. They were prepared to wait for mañana. At the time of writing 55 plus years later, we are still waiting. Within four months of his election Albert met the British Ambassador to Madrid, Sir John Balfour (O 9).

After World War II ended, he proposed to Governor Kenneth Anderson (O 5), that a victorious Britain could lay down conditions to an impoverished Spain. He believed that we had a right to live in Gibraltar, which had not been covered by other treaties. "The time is now, when Britain is strong and victorious" was my father's political approach when seeing the Governor. One or more members of the A.A.C.R. disagreed with his views: "Britain will always be strong and Spain weak". The colonial divide and rule concept had begun. A great opportunity was thus missed, which in all probability might have been successful.

On October 18 1944, Franco sent a personal and confidential letter to the British Prime Minister . . . . In it he expressed his desire to 'clear up' relations between Spain and Britain in a 'sincere, frank and direct' manner in view of the 'serious situation in Europe' and in view of the 'atmosphere of suspicion and hostility towards Spain that exists in Great Britain'. It was a question of whether Stalin's communism, which was now creeping into Italy, France and Greece should succeed, or Britain's acceptance of Franco as 'the Prudent Caudillo of Peace'. 'England has only one other nation on the continent to turn to: Spain'.

NORTH FRONT RACECOURSE E.

A.A. Danino, ESQ.   L. J. Imossi, ESQ.   J.J. Russo, ESQ., O.B.E., J.P.   L.T. COL. J. C. A. Dowse, M.C.   ENG. CAPT. P.D. Fulford, R.N.   I.R. Massias, ESQ.   A.R. Isola, ESQ. J.P.   A.C. Carrara, ESQ., C.M.G., K.C.J.P.,   BRIG. THE HON W.T. Brooks, M.C.,   H.E. THE GOVERNOR (PATRON). Marquis of Marzales. M.R.H. (VICE-PATRON).   J. Bañasco. ESQ.   P.G. Russo, ESQ.

Patron, Vice-Patron and Stewards, Civilian Racing Club, Gibraltar. *(1935-36)*.

Members of the Mediterranean Racing Club.

Albert R. Isola with some of the Jockey Club stewards *(1937)*.

Rosita Baglietto with Isola brothers *(1938)*.

Bolero *(1939)*.

E.

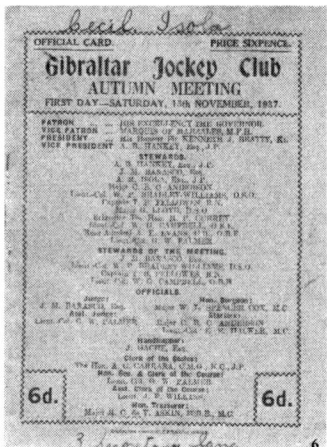

Race card.

Albert Isola - Starter.

They "Re Off".

Carmen Baglietto.

Steward's Cup.

Mediterranean Racing Club and Gibraltar Jockey Club badges.

Gibraltar in the thirties
1.- Passenger's Pier.
2.- Mala Punta.
3.- Hackney carriages.

To face these dangers, it was necessary to 'forget the prejudices' derived from the World War, put an end to 'rivalries and desires to dominate', and 'arrive at an understanding between European countries'. To do this, 'the mutual friendship and co-operation between Great Britain and Spain was necessary', given that the alternative was a 'healthily strategically located' nation with the 'courage and energy' to help Britain maintain peace and security in Western Europe. (El País newspaper)

Churchill's three principles which he addressed to Anthony Eden and which would be reflected in British politics in the immediate post-war period, was generally applicable in Europe and specifically to Spain.

1. Opposition to Communism.
2. Non-intervention in the internal affairs of countries that have not bothered us.
3. No special commitment in Europe that requires the maintenance of a large army.

Had my father's visionary attitude not been locally opposed, many of the political problems that were to follow years later, could probably have been averted.

Adelaide Murto

My mother Adelaide (Lali) Murto, was the second daughter of Matias Murto and Magdalene Bellamy; her sisters were Kittita and Mema. All three were the best of friends and their friendship remained solid throughout their lives.

The 1920's for them had its fair share of good and bad moments. The marriage of my parents took place in 1924, closely followed by the births of their three children Willie, Lennie and myself at Campamento. In 1926 Lali's mother, Magdalene, was diagnosed with liver cancer with just a few months to live. Treatment at the time was primitive and the adage 'Grin and Bear it' pursued. Pain killers would have been virtually useless, as the more advanced ones would have been unavailable locally. Within a year of her death, her husband's mounting debts, ended in his bankruptcy, and he became persona non grata, in Spain and beyond. Campamento was put up for sale, as was the house, racehorses and all that went with them. At least, we could remain in our house in Campamento since it belonged to the Parodi estate.

The trauma that went with his bankruptcy was rarely mentioned to us children. The reasons given for this debacle was that he overstretched his business finances and losses sustained in the Wall Street crash. The dates did not concur, but I never questioned the reasons until well after my retirement, since at the time they seemed reasonable enough. Yet on many occasions when driving past the 'Principe Alfonso Casino' (B2), my mother warned us of the many dangers that gambling had caused to many innocent parties; no doubt remembering her father's past.

Poverty

The poverty that I saw in pre-1936 Spain was appalling: emaciated children, scantily clad and with bad skin rashes, (impetigo and scurvy). The begging hand was everywhere to be seen and their only way of surviving. My first recollection, which remained firm in my mind, must have occurred when I was three. A boy of about six years was prepared to eat a small live crab, for the penny I had in my hand. I gave him my penny and he crunched the live crab in his mouth, showing the various stages of mastication until completion. With that penny, he bought a loaf of bread.

We had no car to reach our Spanish destinations and depended on the Debono brothers and Eduardo Yome for use of theirs. The latter cornered our private hire car market. They were excellent drivers and none suffered from speed mania. On one occasion, Eduardo forgot to stop at the second Spanish customs post in San Roque. The result, the Guardia Civil drew their pistols and a fatality narrowly averted by my mother's super quick reaction. Eduardo had to reverse, in a 1934 car, on the narrowest of roads for a distance of 200 metres. We were fined.

The Spain that I knew in 1936 consisted of an area, no further than 12 miles from Gibraltar, and restricted to Campamento and Miraflores. We were, of course, blessed by my mother's friends: John and Lily Stagnetto whose children, the ever beautiful Mariola (O9) and her two brothers, Lewis and John, were always in our group of close friends. We were often invited for tea to the Culattos, whose mansion in the Avenida de España faced Gibraltar's west. Their next-door neighbour was my maternal grandmother. My recollections of Spain, other than these areas where we amused ourselves, were of backward, unkempt and extremely poor people and places in virtually every respect.

My Last Day in Democratic Spain: July 1936

My last day in Spain prior to General Franco's take over, was spent at Campamento, playing football. On Saturday 18 July 1936 at around 2 p.m. we heard gunfire in the distance, which we ignored. But by 3.30 p.m. the gunfire was more frequent and was coming nearer. Whilst we continued enjoying our football game, Eduardo suggested that we should return back to Gibraltar, as he was not happy with the sound of gunfire, which was growing louder by the minute. We were not aware, that General Franco had landed his army at Algeciras, 12 miles from Campamento. We drove home at our usual slow pace. At the frontier, we met a large number of people, frantic to enter. The frontier gates were closed. The sentry refused us admission, but fortunately contact with the policeman on duty was established by loud shouting in the only language that the sentry would not understand: Spanish. Within half an hour, the military officer on duty, allowed us to enter, as my father had spoken to a senior military officer. We were back in 'terra firma' and 'libre' (H1, H2).

The next day after mass, we met Teddy Cottrell (later Sir Edward), the British Consul in La Liňea. He reported to us that the rebellious army of General Franco had landed at Algeciras and the 'Moors' now occupied the border town of La Liňea. He had personally witnessed several lorries, loaded with corpses and he believed the Civil War had begun in earnest.

My maternal grandparents' good friends and neighbours, the Culattos were caught unaware, for few Gibraltarians expected Franco's Moroccan regiments to land in Algeciras, and be in the adjoining town of La Liňea, the same day. They left their Campamento house that Sunday morning and drove along the 'Avenida de España' (the road next to the bay) at a slow pace for fear of arousing the Moors, who covered large areas of the town with their machine guns in active positions. The petrified family huddled into the car, with their teenage daughters horrified at what might befall them on their four mile drive to the Gibraltar frontier. They were lucky. Nothing happened! They survived.

For the next four years, we were to be confined to the Rock: Campamento and Miraflores verboten. Unlike the closure of 1964, this one had no effect whatever on our way of life. The principal reason being that we had plenty of open spaces for enjoyment like the North Front racecourse (E7, E8, E9), the Victoria and Alameda Gardens, which were still available for civilian recreational use.

Doctors, Mardi Gras and Victorian Discipline

Doctors in Gibraltar, like elsewhere, were treated as gods, and as gods, few patients questioned their competence or ability. For those who disobeyed their doctor's advice, death was often 'swift'. Old wives tales abounded. I was not a healthy child. It was medically suggested and accepted by my parents, that by drinking the waters of Vichy, France, I would improve (C 5). We travelled there and I drank its waters. However, on my return, I continued to be sick, probably with some of the same viral conditions for which I attended others, decades later. All I remember was excessive sleeping and thirst, with a parched tongue and mouth. The doctor strongly advised fluid restriction as the best means to my eventual recovery. Re-hydration had not yet made its name in medicare. Fortunately, I did not accept his treatment. At every available moment, when those around me temporarily disappeared, I made a quick dash to the bathroom. There I gulped down water, desperately needed, which was probably the main reason for my survival. Temperatures were treated with bed rest, warmth, aspirins and a lot of hope.

On one occasion my temperature refused to subside. The doctor suggested that I probably had 'internal' measles, and all efforts had to be directed in forcing the rash outwardly. To this end the wall facing my bed should be painted red—it was, and the curtains changed to red—they were! Shortly after, the rash appeared—it was out! With this the danger of death dissipated, rapidly. At that time many children died from measles and other infectious illnesses.

Due to the abundance of horses in our area, any infection was treated with great care for fear of attracting the tetanus spore. On one occasion, I fell against a loose tree branch, lying on the road. This resulted in a large abscess above my right eye. It had to be incised at home. The scar still remains. Anaesthetics were not used, as there were none, so I was held down. Surgeon Lockhead was pleased at my good 'behaviour' and called me a 'man'. That was a major compliment and I felt great afterwards. Whilst I could have had it opened under general anaesthetic (ether) at the Colonial Hospital, Mr Lockhead did not recommend it. Infections following operations were frequent, and with them often followed death. The era of antibiotics had not yet arrived. My father's appendix was removed at home. The operating theatre was our sitting room. The dining room table was the operating table. He survived the anaesthetic and no infection occurred post-operatively—a great success. My mother, on the other hand, had a breast cancer, in her early thirties. It could not be surgically removed at home, and Surgeon Lockhead referred her to London. The operation was a bigger success for she survived another 55 years, until she died from old age.

Despite hospital infections, there was no place in Europe that had its streets as clean, as Gibraltar had. We were still in the horse-cabby (E 10) and Calpe Hunt era, and many of the stables lay within our city walls. The streets were washed thrice daily with sea-water and were spotlessly clean despite the daily 'goings on' of the horses.

Everything at home followed Victorian values. Sunday was our day of rest, and we all looked forward to attending mass at the Cathedral of St Mary the Crowned. It was obligatory for those of us, over seven, since we had now reached the age of reasoning. I enjoyed it. Sunday lunch was at my grandparents' house. Our bowels were 'clean' for that event, for Friday at 8 p.m. was purgation night. It consisted of the most disgusting medicines I was ever to taste: Black Draught or Castor Oil. It required both my parents 'co-operation' for their sons resisted the potion vehemently, and nose-holding was an essential part, if the weekly cleansing was to be achieved satisfactorily. Mens Sana—Mens Corpora was locally translated into a healthy bowel, healthy body. The weekly flush and other such routines were not peculiar to the Gibraltarians. It was routine everywhere, if you could afford the price of the laxatives. At Stonyhurst progress had left its mark, for there was a choice between Syrup of Figs, and Milk of Magnesia. It was less disgusting, and given on a regular basis if one was in constipation mode for one day: an improvement on home. But unlike home, strict discipline made it a 'grin and bear it' episode, and a 'thank you matron', insisted upon!

Montagu Pavilion

From the 1 April to 1 September, we swam at Montagu Bathing Pavilion, arriving there shortly after 8.00 a.m. The pavilion faced the Admiralty waters and had a central jetty reserved for families only. The southern jetty was for ladies, and all wore full-length black bathing costume (the fashion) to cover their voluptuous figures. All were overweight. The males had the north jetty from which to swim. Sex segregation was absolute and strictly enforced. The only possible way for a male-female encounter was to meet on the anchored raft; located a fair distance from the jetties and in very deep water. The caretakers would not have been amused at such meetings and any female that swam the distance would have been in full glare of the males ashore. The male jetty was closer to the raft. We all had to swim to the raft accompanied by my father. On our return home via the American War Memorial, a full English breakfast awaited us at 9.15 a.m.

But not all was Victorian discipline. On many occasions we had unwanted guests at home and when they came, they came as a pack: the apes. When this occurred, as it often did, 3 Secretary's Lane became a fortress, as they perched high on our Magnolia tree. Windows and doors were firmly closed, and no courtesy appetizers were ever offered. Without food they left, usually by night, though they often knocked at our windows in the hope that they might be welcomed. We knew what would happen if they gained admission. On one occasion, a young ape caused mayhem, destruction and panic within the household until he 'escaped'.

Despite the poverty in the adjoining town of La Liñea, the annual fair and Mardi Gras were enjoyable events, until Franco assumed power. On one occasion, my father egged on by his friends, challenged a 'mini bull' at the La Liñea bull ring, and received the cuts and bruises in his failed 'torero' attempt. He learnt, not from the scolding my mother gave him, but by the shock of his being trampled. Such bravado never returned. Mardi Gras not only ceased in Spain with Franco, but in Gibraltar as well, but for different reasons. Our reason was 'security'! In the Assembly Rooms, a monthly masked ball was held. It was very well attended by the civilian population until the outbreak of World War II. Masks could only be removed outside the rooms. At home our annual fancy dress party ended around that time (C1).

Christmas Day was a family celebration at my grandparents' home. We observed Epiphany as the day in which the Three Kings visited the infant Christ with gifts. It was also our day of the year, for the Three Kings lavished us with all the presents that money could buy. Santa Claus for us came later, in Christmas 1940, during our enforced wartime military evacuation. By then I was old enough not to believe that the Three Kings had specifically come to Gibraltar to give us gifts.

A Day to Remember

The one and only wedding reception that I attended prior to my sister in 1948, was held at home. It took place on 4 July 1934, when Tuto married my Aunt Mema. It was marred by a small incident. Prior to the toast, the bridegroom could not be found. He was consoling my brother Peter, who was five years old, and had drunk a cup of champagne and was partially inebriated, and sat in the garage's corner: sobbing. The same would have happened to me, but the cup of yellow lemonade was snatched from my hand, before I could taste the liquid.

As the Italia liner 'Vulcania' was due to depart for Italy that afternoon for the first stage of the newly-weds' honeymoon, the speeches were kept short and to the point. Lily Imossi, director of Carrara & Co and the Italia Line's agent, led the party on board the tender 'Mary Claire', for the final farewell was to be made from there. Lily, who was Tuto's cousin, accompanied them on board and needless to add, spoke to the captain about the newly-weds. At 8.15 p.m., that evening, the head waiter went to their cabin and escorted them to the darkened dining room. On their arrival the lights went fully on, the diners stood up, and with a thunderous applause, welcomed the newly-weds. During dinner, they were asked to lead the diners to the dance floor, and to the music of Al Jolson's 'Night We Were Wed'. What they hoped would be a quiet honeymoon, turned out to be a public event. They enjoyed it!

Murder

Not all was pleasure in my pre-civil war years. One experience I had, centred on a murder that took place in Market Lane in 1932. My late father had been asked by the Attorney General to assist him in the prosecution. He led the team. The result 'Opisso' was found guilty of murder, and sentenced to be hanged. Our Cathedral was stormed by protestors, and the military were sent from Casemates Square with baseball bats to control, what in effect was an anti-hanging riot. Following Opisso's trial and hanging at Moorish Castle, the Commissioner of Police received enough information to believe that Albert's two youngest children were in grave danger, as a result of the verdict. Gibraltar's most respected Detective Sgt. Ernest Gilbert; (later Superintendent) was delegated to protect us. He was armed. Whenever we left the house, Sgt. Gilbert (C4) was there. When the commissioner felt the danger had passed,

Sgt. Gilbert was withdrawn from what must have been a boring and strenuous exercise. Security at home was raised to 'Red', and this was noticeable. No reasons were given or asked for, until we discovered all when we were older.

Years later, after World War II, I listened to my father and Juror Angel Rugeroni (now a J.P.) discussing the Opisso case. Both agreed that the verdict was the correct one and beyond reproach. During the war, further executions took place, but on Britain's abolition of the death penalty, we followed suit. As a boy I was strongly advised to avoid Market Lane. In 1957, as a young doctor, I was asked to attend a night-call, in the very house where the murder had taken place, and I shuddered. Vivid memories, badly lit staircases and all that can bring a fertile mind to life again, occurred. Fortunately the patient and I had a personality clash, and I was never called there again. Thankfully!

Some years later, I watched the departure of Haile Selassie of Abyssinia (C4), Lion of Judah from Gibraltar. He was given a hero's departure, with a full military Guard of Honour, which stretched from Government House, to Governor's Wharf. It was to be the last time, that I would see senior military officers on horse-back and fully plumed.

With an aunt, as intellectual as Kittita was; willing to impart her knowledge; my early years were filled with good information. She was always prepared to sit down and explain things in-depth. I had a fair understanding, by age nine of major events: World War I; the Wall Street Crash; the Spanish Flu and maritime disasters such as the Titanic and Lusitania. She would take us to the races but rarely backed a horse. Not only would she take us on long walks, but to interesting football matches. One such was a triangular football match, between the Combined Services, Gibraltar United and a La Liñea selection. In this rivalry, spectators naturally supported their own teams. But when the Gibraltarians played against the Spaniards, the services supported them, as indeed the Gibraltarians supported the Spaniards when playing the services. I was too young to understand the reasons, but I had a fair idea that all was not well between the services and the civilian population.

Chapter 3

THE SPANISH CIVIL WAR 1936

My Life Changes Dramatically

My life changed dramatically from day one of the Civil War. I was now allowed to cycle with my brother Peter in town. There were virtually no cars on the roads, so cycling (D2-4) was fairly safe in the lower town area. We were forbidden to ride our bicycles on any hill. The punishment was the sale of our cycles. The brakes would not have withstood the friction necessary for a full stop down our steep hills. We understood as we knew of a child who had died this way on Trafalgar Hill.

My friends Joe, Charlie and Tony Gaggero, Tony Cottrell, Mickey Bowen, Joseph Patron and others enjoyed cycle racing in Ragged Staff (D4). The train locomotive that plied between a small dock next to the R.G.Y.C., the Torpedo Camber and the Dockyard, was the only danger to our enjoyment. Ragged Staff ended some 100 yards north of the yacht club. We rarely saw a car or lorry on the road, since it ended in a cul de sac. It was a perfect area for cycle racing. There was no land reclamation west of the Great War Memorial. The fleet was too large for the Admiralty Harbour to be reclaimed.

The Great War Memorial Steps formed the main landing stage for the thousands of sailors entering town; best seen when the Mediterranean and Home fleets (H12) met in early March (H12). The Mediterranean colour of light from the dark grey of the Home Fleet, distinguished the fleets. The drunkenness and brawls between rival ships' crews was commonplace. The honky-tonks did financially well during the pre-war years. There was no reporting of civilians clashing with the sailors. I kept well away from Main Street, for there was no reason in my childhood days to be there, though on occasion, I saw the merriment that alcohol infuses in a youthful sailor. When fights occurred, the best one could do was to move on. They became like whirlpools, sucking the onlookers and others into the brawl, especially at the times, when the two fleets met.

The North Front Racecourse (E) and the Victoria Gardens became our post-1936 area for physical enjoyment. Cycling and picnicking, in and around our racecourse was great fun. On Saturdays there was horse racing, held either by the Mediterranean Racing Club (M.R.C.) or the Jockey Club (E). Segregation was best seen in these clubs for the M.R.C. was more civilian in every way, whereas the Jockey Club was more service representative.

Swimming at Sandy Bay was reserved for the military officers and their families, and was enforced. The Rock Hotel had its own Lido and private beach, which was reserved for its clients. It adjoined the north side of Sandy Bay. The type of client that sought the comforts of 'The Rock' preferred their evening cocktails to swimming at the Lido. As my father was the hotel's legal advisor, he obtained the necessary permits for the Stagnettos and us to be allowed to swim there. In effect for the next three years, this was our preferred swimming area. Whilst Sandy Bay was reserved for the officers and their families, few availed themselves of this privilege. There was no bus service to the beach and few had cars. Walking in the heat was counter-productive if your reason for swimming was cooling.

One who did own a car was my Uncle Tuto. He had a two-seater Ford with an extra two seats in the boot, big enough for Peter and me to fit. The car required a manual crank for starting or a physical push. The era of starter motors was still sometime away. The Eastern Beach Road was about one kilometre or more long and stretched from Devil's Tower Road to the frontier fence. There was no airport then. At the fence you turned left to the well-tended Victoria Gardens. On one occasion my Great Aunt Clementine noticed a car-wheel racing ahead of us. As my uncle's car had no rear mirror, we looked back to identify the car with the problem. There was none. It was us. She refused to get out of the car until we fixed the wheel. So we did. She declined further outings until Tuto bought a new car, an impossible at the time.

IN ABSENTIA
SUPREME COURT. GIBRALTAR

The trial of Captain Scott of the S.S. Stancroft, was held at Gibraltar on the 10th June 1938. The ship was arrested for contravening the Merchant Shipping Act (carriage of munitions to Spain) by H.M.S. Devonshire on the 9th May 1938 and escorted to Gibraltar. My late father Albert. R. Isola was the Counsel for the Crown. The case received world-wide publicity as the result of the Civil War.

CHARGE OF CARRYING ARMS TO SPAIN

CASE AGAINST BRITISH SHIPMASTER

FROM OUR CORRESPONDENT

GIBRALTAR, JUNE 10

The hearing of the case against Captain Stanley Scott, master of the British steamer Stancroft, who is charged with carrying goods contrary to the Merchant Shipping (Carriage of Munitions to Spain) Act, 1936, was resumed to-day in the Police Court. Mr. D. N. Pritt, K.C., and Mr. G. H. Bing are appearing for the defence. The Spanish Republican Government is also represented.

That part of the Stancroft's cargo in question is stated to consist of nine aeroplane engines and empty cartridge and shell cases. Revenue officers gave evidence of searching the cargo and finding the articles.

The defence has been given leave to inspect the articles seized, which are stored in the naval stores.

GIBRALTAR, June 10.—Captain Scott to-day entered a plea of "Not Guilty."

Counsel for the prosecution, Mr. Albert Isola, said that the prohibited articles referred to included 17 cases of empty cartridge cases, one case of empty shells, and nine aircraft engines.

When the Stancroft was taking in cargo at Barcelona on May 4, confirmed counsel, the Non-Intervention Observer and another official told the defendant that prohibited articles were being loaded, and a list, together with a letter of protest, was handed to him. On the following day the master was again warned that aeroplane engines were being placed in the ship, but he took no notice. The taking in of cargo continued on May 6, and the Stancroft sailed from Barcelona on May 7. Valencia roadstead was reached during the day, and the Stancroft remained there during the day, going to sea every night.

On May 9 an officer from the cruiser Devonshire was ordered to board all British vessels in Valencia. When he reached the Stancroft he asked permission to search the ship, but the defendant said that would be impossible, as it would mean discharging the bulk of the cargo, including a deck cargo of motor-car bodies. The officer returned to the cruiser and later revisited the Stancroft. During this visit Captain Scott produced an empty cartridge case which had fallen from a package broken during the loading operations at Barcelona. The officer then ordered him to proceed to Gibraltar with his ship.

Mr. Pritt, for the defence, asked who had given orders that nobody was to be allowed to go ashore from the Stancroft when she first arrived at Gibraltar, and why a counsel for the defence was not allowed to go on board. The ship's cargo, he said, was about 1,600 tons, of which about 10 tons was now in question. During the loading of the vessel at Barcelona the town was almost continuously bombed by German and Italian aeroplanes, and in those circumstances a mistake was easily made. The case of shells contained an odd lot of about 15, all imperfect and badly packed. They were like a jumble sale lot rather than a serious shipment.

Technical evidence was given by Captain Turnbull, of the Royal Army Ordnance Corps, and Flight Lieutenant Dixon, R.A.F., and the case was then adjourned till Monday.—*Exchange*.

Carrying of arms to Spain
The Times
10th June 1938.

LAW BATTLE IN GIBRALTAR

ALLEGED ARMS FOR SPAIN

Skipper on Trial at Gibraltar

GIBRALTAR, June 10.

The prosecution alleged that empty shell cases and aeroplane engines had been found on board the British steamer Stancroft when the case against the Stancroft's skipper, Captain Stanley Scott, was resumed here to-day in a packed court. Captain Scott, who is accused of carrying arms to Spain, pleaded not guilty. He is being defended by Mr. D. N. Pritt, K.C., who came from London to represent him. Mr. Geoffrey Bing, also of London, and Mr. Sergius Triay, of Gibraltar.

Opening the case for the prosecution to-day, Mr. Albert Isola, a Gibraltar barrister, said that the prohibited articles found on board the Stancroft included 17 cases of empty cartridges, one case of empty steel gun shells, and nine aircraft engines, which are prohibited under section one of the recent Merchant Shipping Act.

Army and Air Force experts gave evidence. Captain Leslie Turnbull, of the R.A.O.C., said he had examined the empty shells and formed the opinion that they could be used as shells if they were filled and fused. Likewise, the empty cartridges found would be useful for making cartridges. Lieutenant James Dixon, of the R.A.F., said the engines were definitely aircraft engines. After these two witnesses had been cross-examined the hearing was adjourned until Monday.

The Stancroft was stopped on May 9 by H.M.S. Devonshire outside Valencia as the result of a report from a non-intervention officer.—Press Association Foreign Special.

BRITISH SEAMEN'S PROTESTS

A protest at the Government's attitude towards the bombing of British ships in Spanish ports was made yesterday by Mr. W. R. Spence, general secretary of the National Union of Seamen. There was apprehension and alarm among seafarers, Mr. Spence stated, at the supine attitude of the British Government towards the safety of merchant seamen in Spanish waters.

British seamen had been bred in the tradition that sailing under the British flag was a safe and sure protection in every sense. To-day they were beginning to look upon the flag more with contumely than with respect. "At least six of my members," he added, "have been killed and many injured in Spanish Government ports by insurgent 'planes and the correspondence I am receiving from the relatives of the deceased and injured men is hardly complimentary to the British Government."

Mr. Spence said that seamen felt that if the life of one British seaman had been sacrificed statesmen such as Salisbury, Gladstone, or even Lloyd George would have taken drastic action and damned the consequences. "Something must be done. The Government heads are behaving like Nero."

Alleged arms for Spain
Manchester Guardian 10th June 1938.

IN ABSENTIA   G.
SOME OF THE HEADINGS.

BRITON ON 'ARMS FOR SPAIN' CHARGE
Socialist K.C. in Court Duel

Daily Mail 11th June 1938.

German denounced British captain
GIBRALTAR, Monday.

Daily Express 14th June 1938.

German Control Man's Duel with K.C.
"WERE YOU HOSTILE TO BRITON?"
From G. V. JAMES

Daily Mail 14th June 1938.

Gibraltar Trial
"GERMAN INSULTED ROYAL FAMILY"
BY A SPECIAL CORRESPONDENT

Daily Herald 14th June 1938.

BRITISH SKIPPER ON TRIAL
No-Case Plea
CHARGE OF CARRYING ARMS TO SPAIN

Manchester Guardian 14th June 1938.

"NAVY DID NOT HELP"
GIBRALTAR, Tuesday.
MR. D. N. PRITT, K.C., M.P., attacked foreign propaganda in Gibraltar court today for suggesting that British ships off Spain were contraband runners and were not entitled to naval protection.

Daily Express 15 June 1938.

BRIBE STORY AT "SPANISH SHIP" TRIAL

Daily Mirror June 1938.

BRITAIN ENCOURAGES PIRATES — Says K.C.
BY OUR OWN CORRESPONDENT

Daily Herald 15th June 1938.

'STOP CASE,' URGES K.C. IN SPAIN ARMS TRIAL
From G. V. JAMES

Daily Mail June 1938.

IN ABSENTIA
A FEW INTERESTING BITS.

G.

DEFENCE OF STANCROFT'S CAPTAIN

PROSECUTION CRITICIZED
FROM OUR CORRESPONDENT
GIBRALTAR, JUNE 14

When the hearing of the charge against Captain Scott, of the Stancroft, was resumed to-day, Mr. D. N. Pritt, K.C., in a four-hour address submitted legal arguments and asked for the immediate dismissal of the case on the grounds that the evidence of the only two witnesses to the facts—namely, the German Non-Intervention observer, Captain Hintze, and the second mate, Mr. Travers—was most unreliable and contradictory, and not only

The Times 15th June 1938.

Were you very angry about this protest against trampling on the British flag by Hitler and Mussolini?—I know nothing about that.

Mr. Pritt: Did someone aboard show you an English newspaper with a picture of the Royal Family, and did you say, 'This Royalty makes me vomit'?—I don't remember. I respect every nationality.

Mr. Pritt: Did you endeavour to prevent shell-cases going aboard?—No, I've no right.

Daily Mail 14th June 1938.

Mr. Pritt then told the court that he intended to take action, through diplomatic channels, to secure the release of the Stancroft's general cargo, which included a large consignment of hospital beds. This cargo, he claimed, had been detained by the Crown with no legal right.

Daily Mail 15th June 1938.

GIBRALTAR, Monday.

QUESTIONS about Nazi propaganda on the London steamer Stancroft and insults to the British Royal Family were put to a German non-intervention officer when the trial of the vessel's skipper, Captain Stanley Scott, was resumed here to-day.

Daily Herald 14th June 1938.

K.C.'s "I Protest"
From Daily Mail Correspondent
GIBRALTAR, Wednesday.

"I protest," cried defending counsel, Mr. D. N. Pritt, Socialist M.P. and K.C., jumping to his feet during the arms case to-day, when Mr. Albert Isola, prosecuting, alleged that the defence had sought to make political capital.

Daily Mail 16th June 1938.

Replying to this submission to-day, Mr. Albert Isola, the Crown counsel, said that there was ample evidence to establish a prima facie case and that Capt. Scott was privy to a contravention of the Act.

The court adjourned until Friday, when a decision will be given on Mr. Pritt's contention.

Meanwhile, Capt. S. L. Spence, Second Officer Isaacson, and a new crew for the Stancroft have arrived here on board the P. & O. liner Strathmore.

It is understood that Capt. Scott, who is ill, is waiting to go on holiday.

Daily Telegraph 16th June 1938.

---

*Fourteen months later,
both governments were at war.*

Fishing in the Bay

Despite the Civil War raging just across the border, we used our beautiful bay. With an uncle like Tuto and his brother George Imossi, we knew we could rely on them for the use of their two shipping agents' launches, the Aquilon and Samarang. Both were directors of the old established firm of Mateos. "Whenever you want to use the launch, give me one day's notice", stated Tuto.

The hook and sinker was all we required, for within half an hour I could fill a full bucket with fish, as all others on board could similarly do (D8). There was no oil pollution in the bay; just fine coal dust floating, which was blown on to the Spanish beaches. Fish was plentiful and the 1960's era of Spanish over fishing had not yet begun. Swimming on these trips was not permitted, since none of us, once in the water, could have got back on board, as there was no ladder. Other shipping agents followed and regular fishing parties were enjoyed throughout the summer. What was interesting with hindsight was the lack of safety equipment on board, for had we needed the use of lifejackets, we would have been in serious trouble. There was one shipping agent who outperformed all. It was Bland's. The Gaggeros were not only shipping agents; they also owned the 'Rescue.' Two or three times a year, Mabel Gaggero gave a party for Marilou and Joe's friends. The 'Rescue' was a salvage tug, large enough for us to run around, with an accommodation ladder, which was lowered to the swimmers' level. Swimming in the bay was thus possible. It was far more refreshing and exhilarating than that experienced from the shore. The day's main event was to watch Captain Ritchie dive from the bridge and swim under the ship's hull from one side to the other in seconds. Capt. Ritchie was my father's shipping advisor. Later, he and his son, both pilots, made my life as port doctor easier. It was appreciated.

Education

Not all was pleasure. My brother Willie, prior to Stonyhurst was a pupil at the Line Wall Christian Brothers School, and my sister Lennie, prior to entering Farnborough Hillside Convent, was a pupil at the Loreto Convent. Both these schools were excellent establishments and were managed by the Irish. The religious orders took their vows seriously and as a result many Gibraltarians benefited greatly from their education. Unlike the English public schools, Latin was not taught, so without Latin, the pupils being Catholic and colonial, most would have had difficulties at the university admission level. As a result many Catholics, before 1914, sought university education in Ireland. For reasons unknown to me, my early years had not been spent at Line Wall, but educationally, I had the benefits of Kittitas's superior knowledge, which she generously imparted to my young mind. Years later, I found what she taught me very useful, when discussing a plethora of subjects at university level.

In 1936, and with two years to go before entering Hodder (K1), the preparatory school of Stonyhurst, I could neither read nor write. The three Rs of education; reading, riting and rithmetic, were absent from my curriculum. To counter this, my father engaged an excellent teacher by the name of Ernest Britto (D1). His daunting task was to make us literate before we left for Hodder; and two years was all the time he had. We had one hour of evening classes and one or two hours of unsupervised homework. Mr Britto needed patience, a lot of it, and indeed he appeared to have oodles of it;

for by the time we left for Hodder, I could read, write, spell and was good at arithmetic.

With hindsight and medical knowledge, my body fluids and brain parts must have been saturated with the poison lead. My soldiers, toys, paints, drinking water pipes etc. were of lead or contained large amounts of the substance. One of my hobbies was melting lead and casting it into soldiers. All warships were bottom cleaned at the dockyard and their lead paint scrapings would have entered the food chain. Fish was the mainstay of protein for all residents. Yet despite all this, I did not appear to be mentally affected, for I achieved the 3 Rs by the time I was ten!

Spanish Civil War

The Spanish Civil War and our partially closed border did not affect many Gibraltarians. The Calpe Hunt and other Spanish sports' activities were temporarily suspended. The brutality of the Civil War was well reported by the B.B.C. World Service and the Gibraltar Chronicle through its arrangement with Reuter's News Agency. There were no local television stations or radio to switch on and many details of the macabre Civil War atrocities were spread locally by bush telegraph. Those readers, who went to Sacarello's News agency, were able to buy their U.K. dailies on average, eight days later: 'Some news was better than no news at all'.

Four Maritime Events—One Legal

There were three maritime events, during the Spanish Civil War, which I witnessed indirectly, since the three warships arrived in port, and could easily be seen from the Look Out at 3 Secretary's Lane. They were the destroyer H.M.S. Hunter, which had struck a mine off Almeria and nearly sunk. She was towed back to Gibraltar by the cruiser Arethus and docked at the dockyard. Three sailors were buried at North Front after their bodies were carried on gun-carriages through Gibraltar's Main Street. It was a sad and impressive event.

German Pocket Battleship: Deutschland (H5-9)

Two weeks later, the German pocket battleship, Deutschland arrived in Gibraltar on Sunday 30 May 1937. Two republican bombers had dropped two bombs; one hit the side of the warship and yet caused no casualties and the other hit the ratings' mess, killing 23 men wounding 80 more. The Deutschland was in a restricted war zone area off the island of Ibiza. Germany, though not involved directly in the Civil War, was a supporter of Franco. At home, we knew that the Deutschland was speeding 'full ahead' to Gibraltar, through my Uncle Tuto, whose brother George was the German Vice-Consul, and was in constant touch with the German Embassy in London. He gave us a daily and sometimes, bi-daily, running commentary of what was actually happening in London's German Embassy, which was keeping the Mateos agents so fully engaged.

I was unable to see the battleship steam in through the southern entrance, as we were all attending the Corpus Christi procession. The battleship berthed near the Dockyard Tower with its flag at half-mast, as were the flags of all British warships in Admiralty Harbour shortly after. Fifty-three of the seamen were admitted to the military hospital, some of whom died during the night.

Gibraltar's leading undertaker, H. Codali Ltd, was given instructions to arrange for the burials of the dead within 24 hours of their arrival, as is required by our health laws. The company's workshop toiled day and night to complete the coffin order for the burial ceremony next day, which was to take place at the North Front Cemetery. For some unknown reason, the Deutschland sailed before the funeral took place, but left the chaplain and an interpreter behind.

I watched the procession from the Causeway. Each military lorry carried two coffins draped with the German Nazi flag, except the last two coffins, which were covered with wreaths. It was said, that there were not enough flags to cover all the coffins. Large crowds attended the funeral procession including senior military figures, and George Imossi, as the German Consul. To me, aged nine, it appeared to be a never-ending procession, but out of curiosity I stayed to the end. The majority of the servicemen attending were British.

The same evening, the German pocket battleship, Admiral Scheer, accompanied by four destroyers pounded Almeria for two long hours, a case of an-eye-for-an-eye was about to take place between 'neutral' countries. It was shortly after that, when Peter and I became witnesses, to an immovable object: the Governor and a determined dictator: Adolf Hitler. Within days of the burials, a request for the seamen's exhumation arrived at George Imossi's office. The German Consul was perplexed by such a request, for under our public health laws no person can be exhumed within a year of burial. What in effect, the German Embassy was requesting, was simply a breach of our public health laws; and in a fortress governed by a military man: General Harrington. The first answer given by the Governor was a diplomatic 'no', and in less diplomatic terms, 'over my dead body'. Tuto was privy to all the communications between Von Ribbentrop (the German Ambassador to London) and his brother George, since they both worked and owned the Mateos office and shipping agency. For the next few days, Tuto kept us well informed of all that was going on at his office. Progress was nil, and Von Ribbentrop was informed of the public health law that forbade exhumation until one year had elapsed. 'The law is the law' said the Governor. As they spoke, the pocket battleship Deutschland was on course here to collect its dead. Von Ribbentrop would not take 'no' for an answer. Further exchanges took place in the next days. In the last one, the German Embassy informed George that the exhumations had to take place, for Adolf Hitler wanted a state funeral in Germany for its dead. Whilst George, in Gibraltar tried hard but could go no further, Hitler had better luck. Directly, or indirectly (via Von Ribbentrop) a call to Prime Minister Neville Chamberlain produced the required result; for shortly afterwards, the order to disinter was made by Governor Harrington. This was one appeasement that was never recorded.

Since the burials, 'Hardly had 10 days gone by' wrote Codali, 'when the ministry gave instructions for exhumations of the bodies and their transportation to Germany. The exhumations were carried out during the night, with the aid of army searchlights, and the bodies laid to rest in specially sealed coffins, and into packing cases. They were duly taken on board the Deutschland before her departure'.

We followed Tuto's advice, and went to the Causeway where we once again witnessed the second funeral procession. It was nothing like the first, and the number of onlookers was now much reduced.

The procession disappeared from view, as they turned into an area now occupied by White's Marina. From there they were transferred by lighter to the Deutschland, where a Guard of Honour awaited them. The ship sailed on the same day as the exhumations. Two of the gravediggers were reported to have died but this could not be confirmed. When the injured German seamen recovered and were fit for hospital discharge, two of their warships called at Gibraltar: the Admiral Graf Spee and the Nurnberg; the latter taking the remaining patient sailors from the military hospital. Three months later, the pocket battleship Admiral Scheer arrived and following a tea party on board, presented the 'Order of the German Red Cross' to many of those medical officers, military sisters and nurses associated with the treatment of the injured, including General Harrington. Amongst the Gibraltarians were George Imossi, Adela Giraldi and Nurse Canto. The latter was an outstanding nurse, and one who could easily have been named as the Gibraltarian nurse of the 20th Century. I know, I saw her work. She was so dedicated, it was unbelievable.

My uncle gave me the headbands of the Deutschland, Graf Spee and Admiral Scheer, which I kept in my playroom for some years. When war broke out, in a fit of childish nationalism, I threw them into the wastepaper basket; a pity in retrospect. The Graf Spee was later scuttled in the River Plate, off Montevideo, after engaging Cruiser H.M.S. Exeter and destroyers Achilles and Ajax. I watched this battle on Movietone news in a Gibraltar cinema. The war was not going well for Britain and the sinking of the Graf Spee made us all extremely happy. Years later, I was told that the bombing of the Deutschland had been a case of mistaken identity. The 'Reds' were after Franco's flagship Canarias and the attack was carried out by two U.S.S.R. pilots.

The question of whether the German Red Cross medals could be worn by the military had to be vetted by King George VI. It was allowed, as it was a humanitarian decoration. Admiral Carls, prior to the award ceremony thanked 'Governor Harrington on behalf of the Fűhrer and the German Government . . . . ' In the last paragraph of his letter to the German Admiral, Harrington wrote: 'To me this honour has an added sentiment. I finish my active career in a few months and I shall always treasure the fact that the last honour I can receive comes from the nation for which I have the most profound respect'.

Two years and two weeks later both countries were at war!

H.

Refugees denied entry. About 600 made it.

Refugees denied exit. Machine guns further down.

Weeping, She Sank With Ship

By PATRICK FORREST

TERROR, stark and swift, during the torpedoing of the British steamer Endymion was re-lived for me yesterday when I heard the first full story of the sea outrage from Chief Engineer W. Wood, of Stafford-road, Cardiff, one of the four survivors, at first believed to have perished.

As 34-year-old W. Wood talked to me by telephone from the office of the British Consul at Cartagena, in Southern Spain, he brought to my desk in the "Daily Sketch" offices a vivid scene of heroism and pathos.

His last memory of the ship as she went down was that of a woman—28-year-old Mrs. Laura Verano, wife of the skipper.

Chief Engineer Wood heard her calling despairingly for her dog, saw her frantically refusing to leave the ship without her pet, even as seas swept the decks and fire ate through the holds.

"I shall never forget that woman's face as I saw it last," Mr. Wood told me. "Things had happened with a terrible, fantastic swiftness. Men were screaming—some in agony—but Mrs. Verano walked about the decks in her pyjamas. She was shouting above the pandemonium one word 'Buster,' the name of her dog.

ONLY HOPE

"Her only hope was to jump—the lifeboats were disabled—but I saw her wave away offers to get her over the side. Tears streamed down her face as she wandered about the deck looking for the dog.

"As the old ship sank she still searched and called the dog's name. Nothing would have made her leave the ship without it. I think she must have already known that her husband, the skipper, had perished."

The chief engineer had to control his emotions before he could tell me more of the tragedy.

"We were taking a cargo of coal to Cartagena for the Spanish Government," he went on, "and we took care to be well out of the line of trouble. Then at dawn on Monday we moved in at half-speed towards Cartagena. We were about 16 miles south of Cape Tinoso. The sun came up blazing. Suddenly there was a terrific explosion.

"We were not sure whether we had struck a mine or had been torpedoed, till I saw something in the path of the sun. It must have been a submarine, sniping us from the cover of the dawn.

"The ship lurched and I heard the screams of wounded and dying men. We listed badly, then started to sink rapidly by the head.

"The port lifeboat, which had been made ready for emergency, was useless when the falls jammed. It was then I saw Mrs. Verano stalking unhurriedly about the decks, calling her dog. It was unforgettable.

"When I saw it was only a matter of

Capt. Adolfo (Toto). Verano Andlaw.

He Grabbed Boy, Jumped

seconds before we went under I grabbed the cabin boy, Antonio Sarrito, and jumped.

"I saw the mate, Mr. Thomas, leaping, and the mangled body of a member of the crew being dashed against the torn bows of the ship. Water was rushing into No. 2 hold and steam was enveloping everything.

SWAM FOR 45 MINUTES

"Then, for 45 minutes I swam about, clinging to driftwood—I had no lifebelt—and narrowly escaping being drawn under as the Endymion plunged.

"It was deadly cold in the water, and, after seeing the ship go, my memory is just a haze of clinging to driftwood and shouting to other members of the crew who might have been near me in the sea.

"I was picked up, with the mate, the cabin boy and a badly-injured A.B., by a patrol boat. We have just arrived at Cartagena.

"I wish you would tell my young wife in Cardiff that I am absolutely O.K., and that there is nothing for her to worry about."

Daily Sketch, (3rd February 1938).

H.

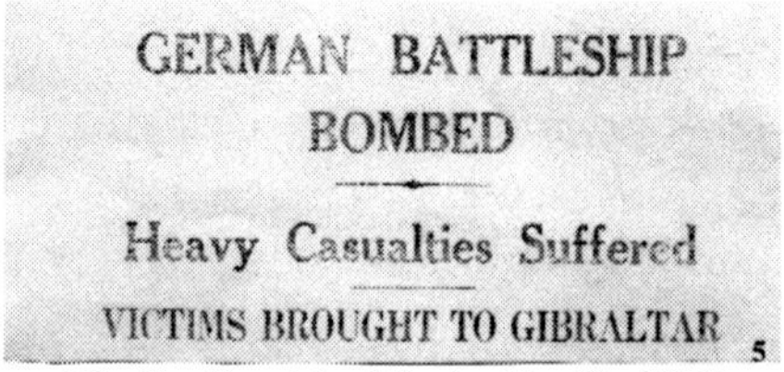

GERMAN BATTLESHIP BOMBED

Heavy Casualties Suffered

VICTIMS BROUGHT TO GIBRALTAR 5

Gibraltar Chronicle. *(Monday May 31st 1937).*

GRAVE INTERNATIONAL SITUATION

Germany's Direct Action

ALMERIA BOMBARDED AS REPRISAL FOR DEUTSCHLAND BOMBING 6

Gibraltar Gazette. *(Tuesday June 1st 1937).*

Deutschland *(1931).* *Photo by: Luis Photos.*

Funeral, North Front.

State Funeral, Wilmenshaven. Adolf Hitler attends.

Jose Luis Diez (Republican) aground in Catalan Bay.
Photo by: C. Culatto.

Admiral Canaris.

Combined Fleets in South Admiralty Harbour. Light grey (Mediterranean Fleet). Dark grey (Home Fleet). A small fraction. *(1936).* *Photo by: C. Culatto.*

Jose Luiz Diez (H10)

One British, one German and now one Spanish destroyer, but this time from the republican side: the Jose Luiz Diez. She had been holed in an encounter with the nationalist fleet, and had sought refuge in Admiralty Harbour, where she was tied to a mooring buoy close to Coaling Island and in full view of our 'Look Out'. She remained there for some months, until one night she slipped her mooring and made a dash for the Mediterranean. A pre-arranged signal by a Franco sympathiser at Europa Point warned the nationalist warships on the east side of the Rock that the Diez was about to run into the Mediterranean. She was pounded as she cornered Europa Point and was deliberately run aground at Catalan Bay, where further shells exploded. One day she was in full view from our house, the next she was aground in Catalan Bay. She did not remain there too long, at least, not long enough for my Kodak box camera to record it from ashore.

British Endymion (H3, H4)

But not all sea visitors were warships; other ships came into the Civil War fray depending on which side you were on, and my father was engaged for some of these cases. The one that had the greatest impact on my family and our friends was the torpedoing of the 'Endymion' bound for the government held port of Cartagena in Southern Spain. She was fully loaded with 1,500 tons of coal, which had been supplied a few days earlier at Gibraltar. She was the first British vessel to be sunk by torpedo. The reaction of the British Government was swift. Four destroyers were sent to identify the submarine, and to sink it, though this was not stated in the press release.

Captain Adolphus Verano, his wife and nine others including a Swedish observer went down with the ship. It was reported at the time, that the wife dashed down to save her dog, and was quickly followed by her husband. The ship heavy with coal sank in four minutes

The captain was the son of the well known doctor Louis Verano. He had six sons and all were professional men. Due to their influence, popularity and charisma, their tragic loss was felt throughout the town. The sinking of the Endymion was often spoken about even years later. Dr Verano's grandchildren still survive, and have had a major influence on the shaping of Gibraltar. The family name of Verano-Andlaw has been shortened to Andlaw, and Louis, Dr Verano's grandson, was elected Vice-President of the Gibraltar Chamber of Commerce in recent times.

Admiral 'Canaris' (H11)

His name was often bandied about in local circles and was probably confused with the 'nationalist' warship Canarias. In 1935, Canaris was made head of Abwer; Germany's equivalent to Britain's MI6. Between 1935-36, he organised a German spy network in Spain. He spoke excellent Spanish. He was the moving force behind the decision that sided Germany with General Franco during the Spanish Civil War, despite the fact that Hitler's initial decision was not to partake in this adventure.

He advised 'Franco not to permit German passage through Spain for the purpose of capturing Gibraltar'. According to written sources 'All of Franco's arguments on this stance were studied and dictated in detail by Canaris. At the same time, as Canaris convinced Franco on this issue, a significant sum of money was deposited by the British into Franco and his Generals' Swiss accounts. Its aim was to convince Franco to be neutral. Spain's infrastructure, roads, railway lines etc. were in a bad way in 1940, as the result of the Civil War. Any army invading Spain at that time would have had major problems in achieving its military objective.

In 1942 Canaris was a regular visitor to Spain. Whilst in Spain, he made contacts with British agents from Spain and Gibraltar. He was anti-communist. His mannerism was that of a gentleman and his behaviour and style would have been incompatible with the thugs in the Nazi Party and Hitler. He planned several coups in Germany against Hitler. All failed. A few weeks before war ended, he was hanged. He was taken to the gallows, barefooted and naked: a traitor to Hitler's cause.

Chapter 4

HODDER PLACE 1938.

WORLD WAR II BEGINS

To England

On the 10 April 1938, on a beautiful spring day, blue sky and a calm sea, I left for Hodder Place, Clitheroe, accompanied by my parents, Aunt Kittita and family friends the Stagnettos. It was my first trip to England. We left from Waterport on board the tender 'Mary Claire', to join the P & O Maloja which lay at anchor in Gibraltar bay. It was on its way to England from the Far East.

Following the lowering of the Quarantine (Q) flag, we boarded the liner and quickly settled. Before the ship sailed, we went to the top deck to bid farewell to our Rock. Large numbers of bum-boats (K 9) were tied to the ship's side, selling their Spanish wares. Within half an hour, the ship's horn blared; three long and one short deafening sounds. The 'Mary Claire' responded and within minutes, the ship began to vibrate as its propellers turned around. We were on our way to England; to school and to see my brother Willie. I was thrilled with the idea of going to school, since I had never been to one. I was now ten and a big boy. As the ship sailed towards the Strait, the Rock visibly shrank by the minute until it eventually disappeared behind the Tarifa Hills of southern Spain.

There was plenty to do on deck and we were quickly told by a steward that priority for deck games was for the over-eighteens. At mealtimes we took the first sitting. The food and service were excellent, as you would expect on pre-war liners' first class. The liner's officers were from Britain. The crew were all Indians and dressed in their imperial uniforms. They were efficient, polite and subservient. Most of the passengers were returning 'home' from their colonial appointments, with a sprinkling of military officers and their families. The impressive evening cocktails were held in the main lounge, prior to the second sitting. The most beautiful women to be seen, young and old, were there. Well positioned near the lounge doors, I had good access to the delicious potato crisps, while the stewards sailed past me, towards the smart revellers. I looked forward to the day that I would be part of that event as a man. But it was not to be, for war broke out, and after the war, these luxury liners were replaced by troopers. The liner was alive with happy passengers, returning from their colonial or military duties, and only days from seeing their loved ones once again. When we reached Cape Finisterre, three days after leaving Gibraltar, the weather changed. Rain, grey skies, and rough seas took hold. The mood became sombre. We had sailed into the Bay of Biscay. The decks lost their human load. The ship began to roll and the restaurant duly emptied. Games on deck ended, and the liner became a ghost ship. This state of affairs continued until we reached Plymouth, when more rain and seagulls welcomed us. After customs, we all boarded a private bus for our long journey to Blackpool. Most of the passengers however stayed on board, for their final destination was London's Tilbury. Those who also disembarked travelled onwards by G.W.R (Great Western Railway), to other destinations.

Blackpool

We arrived in Blackpool late that night exhausted, and in a state of near starvation. As Lancashire is Britain's most friendly county, the staff at the Enville Private Hotel opened their kitchen and fed us with eggs, bacon sausages and chips. It was Good Friday, so more of a choice was unavailable. We were grateful. My parents abstained from all food as was required by church law at the time.

Up early next day, and with the Stagnettos, (K 6) we boarded our private bus: destination Stonyhurst. As the term had not yet finished, Willie, John Haynes and Lewis Stagnetto could not join us for Blackpool that day. They were, however, allowed to lunch with us at the Shireburn Arms (M 8). After lunch Willie returned to Stonyhurst (M 1), as he was partaking of the Easter Steeplechase. We watched him race. He lost!

Accompanied by my parents, we then drove to Hodder Place (K 1), where the Rector, Father McEvoy S. J. showed us around the preparatory school to Stonyhurst. All the boys seemed extremely happy, since it was the school's last day of term. We were shown around and given a good tea. My first impression of school was positive. My father's psychology was working. That evening we returned to Blackpool but without Willie and Lewis, who went back to school.

On Easter Sunday we attended High Mass at St Peter's Church (M 10) where Willie was the boat bearer. Later he took part in the O.T.C.'s Easter Parade. As my father wrote: 'After mass we watched the church parade in the playground, which included a march past'. Having obtained permission from the Rector, Willie was allowed to join us after lunch and leave school half a day early. We all proceeded by bus to Blackpool at about 4.00 p.m.

We remained at Blackpool for 12 glorious and happy days, regularly frequenting the Pleasure Beach, with its upmarket entertainment including the Big Dipper and Fun House. Blackpool Tower, the Winter Gardens, the Palace and its piers also came under our remit. My father wrote 'There was an enormous quantity of playing machines, and a great deal of time was spent there, particularly at the North Pier. Like everything in life, all that is good has an end, and that end came on 26 April, when we boarded the L.M.S. (London Midland and Scottish) train for London's Euston.

To London . . .

We stayed at the Mount Royal in Oxford Street. My mother, Aunt Kitty and my sister Lennie took to shopping, whilst the male side joined my father; swimming in Dolphin Square; ice skating at The Empress Hall and boating on the Serpentine. We went to the musical comedy 'Me and My Gal' and for the first time we went to talking films: 'Snow White and the Seven Dwarfs'; 'Count of Montecristo'; 'Mad about Music' and 'A Yank at Oxford'. In Gibraltar regular sound films were about to make their debut.

We ate at the Trocadero, Café Royal, Martinez and other excellent restaurants. In the first two, if we behaved ourselves and ate our meals, the headwaiter would reward us with a chocolate statuette. We behaved! I watched the Cup Final between Arsenal and Preston N.E. on a black and white television set at the Mount Royal. It was an experimental out-doors trial. The reception was poor and break-downs occurred frequently.

To The Unknown

On Tuesday 10 May, my pre-school holidays came to a sad end. Neither my mother, Kittita or Lennie came to bid us farewell, for they were too emotionally wrought to escort us to Euston station. This did not help. My father accompanied us.

To Hodder (K 1)

On the packed platform, jammed with parents and their children, my father forgot to hand us our railway tickets. That was not a problem, as the ticket collector failed to appear. At 1.30 p.m. on the dot, to visible sobbing, the school train left for Whalley, (the nearest station to Stonyhurst), also calling at Rugby and Crewe, where other boys joined in. Each carriage was reserved for a class and with one Jesuit supervising. My father wrote about our sad farewell, that we had borne it 'with a certain amount of courage'. We knew no one, but as we went northwards, conversations and friendships began. This helped. On arrival at Whalley's railway station, I got my first glimpse of Jesuit organisation. It was superb. Within a short period of time, we were on our way to Hodder by the schoolbus, to serve our first three months as boarders.

On arrival, we were taken to the Refectory for a short evening meal. Then the matron supervised our bath. Afterwards to bed, lights out and more general sobbing. There were two dormitories, one large and one smaller one. I was in the former. It consisted of individual wooden cubicles, all joined together, in four rows with a curtain to allow one some privacy.

The next night, the master came to every cubicle and relieved us of all our sweets. "We don't want mice and rats in the dormitory, do we?" "You have too much; we will give some to the others. Do you agree?" I did, what else could I have done.

The next morning after washing, to Holy Mass, followed by breakfast; lumpy porridge, semi cooked boiled egg, rhubarb and milk ad libitum. There was no fresh milk available in Gibraltar, so I had not acquired that taste early in life. Lunch was no better. Soup that looked more like dish water; roast beef that was grisly and rare, then more rhubarb. By supper time, I was so hungry that I ate whatever was placed in front of me. Most of the boys thought the food was excellent. The policy of sending me in the summer was clear: gradual acclimatization, summer sports and the shortest calendar term. It was cleverly thought out, for I was not to see my parents for 'only' another ten weeks.

To go from a 2 ½ mile enclave, where I could roam fairly freely, to a cage-like existence, is not one that I could easily recommend. With 70 resident boys, all under 12, there was no other solution possible if the Jesuits were not to lose control of their pupils. Within this restricted area, we could play football, cricket, rounders and other games, for the playground lay in front of the school. The sports field and cricket ground were some 50 metres way from the school railings. Class walks were led by the master from behind, thus avoiding a straggler getting lost. Security for the boys was paramount.

On our first sunny day and to the school's general excitement, we were to go to Paradise (K 1). Whilst I associated Paradise with our recent visit to Blackpool, I was soon to learn what it was not. It consisted of the Hodder Valley, which lay below the hill upon which the school was perched and surrounded at its periphery by the Hodder River. A herd of cows grazed on its verdant fields, where two posts identified a rugger pitch (K 1).

Swimming in the river was compulsory, but as I identified myself as a good swimmer, I swam at its deep end. Unaware of the differences between fresh and salt water, I had difficulties with my buoyancy and as a result I gulped water unintentionally. The water was bitterly cold (K 4). That was not my worst shock, for I had never seen a cow, and not knowing the differences between a cow and a bull, kept at a safe distance from all bovine creatures. I had no idea what the distinguishing features were. I kept a close eye, just in case they decided to gore or trample me, as would have been the case in the Spanish scenario.

PREPARING FOR WAR

I.

Departure of His Excellency the Governor
General Sir W. Edmund Ironside
G.C.B., C.M.G., D.S.O., &c.

Mrs. Dooley —
Four Corners   9.30 a

1

General Sir W. Ironside leaves Gibraltar from Four Corners. Odd place to leave. From here to the Western Front to command The B.E.F.

Viola Rugeroni answers the call (1939).

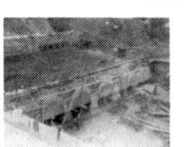

Commercial Square (later John Mackintosh Square). One of the burrows (A.R.P. shelters) in various stages of construction.

2

3

TUESDAY, The Daily Mail, MAY

"The Rock will not be Caught Napping"

DEEP SHELTERS FOR ALL NEARLY READY AT GIB.

Governor's Plans

From NOEL MONKS, Daily Mail Special Correspondent

GIBRALTAR, Monday.

GENERAL SIR EDMUND IRONSIDE, Civil and Military Governor of Gibraltar, discussed with me for an hour to-day his plans for the protection of the Rock's 15,000 civilians in an emergency.

The Governor's constant companions in his office in Government House are two bull-terriers, one of which nestled on his master's lap while we talked of air raids, bombs, and shelters—deep shelters.

Sir Edmund told me that by July underground shelters will be ready for every inhabitant. "They are deep shelters because they are the only kind that are safe," he said. "Nothing man can build above ground will stand a direct hit by a two-tons bomb, but once my people enter their shelters here they will be 100 per cent. safe. I have been fortunate in having A.R.P. experts and engineers who know their job thoroughly—and get on with it.

"The total cost of the shelters will be £100,000. Allowing for the 1,000 wives and children of the garrison who would be sent home and the A.R.P. workers, who would be on duty, the Rock's ten shelters will accommodate 1,500 each, and can be filled within two minutes of the receipt of a warning.

"Rabbit-Burrows"

"We plan to adopt the 'rabbit-in-burrow' system in war-time, when residents will never be far beyond the entrances to the shelters. These people know and realise the dangers of war and they respond sensibly and promptly to all efforts to protect them. The shelters will be fitted with electric light and will be well ventilated.

Sir Edmund explained that the censorship regulations he is bringing in will be purely an emergency measure and will not affect Press messages in peace time. "It is just another of those things which have been left undone," he said. "I believe in getting everything ready before an emergency arrives—not after. If there is one place that is not going to be caught napping again the place is Gibraltar."

State Secret

I asked Sir Edmund about his recent mystery visit to General Nogues, the military commander of French Morocco, but he waved the question aside with "That's a State secret."

It is easy to understand how Sir Edmund has come to be the Rock's most popular Governor in two centuries. His strong, handsome face and tall stature tell of an iron man, and his gentleness to his dogs reveals his kindly, human qualities.

4

THE WORLD IS SAYING WE ARE YELLOW

They Sneer at our Flag!

ONCE upon a time a couple of Spanish Customs officials tore off the ear of Mr. Jenkins.

Robert Walpole had kept England out of the war of the Polish Succession, and only five years earlier had boasted to the Queen that not one Englishman was among the 50,000 slain in Europe in twelve months.

And now the pacifistic Walpole was forced by public opinion to draw the sword.

THAT WAS IN 1739.

✦ ✦ ✦

Once upon a time a mob at Athens injured the property of a Jew, and because that Jew was also a British subject Palmerston turned out our Navy to blockade the Piraeus port. Britain protested.

France nervously offered mediation.

Palmerston was censured by the Lords and by Peel and Gladstone in the Commons.

Exaggerate as the Jew's claim was, Palmerston triumphed with his greatest speech.

"THE WATCHFUL EYE AND THE STRONG ARM OF ENGLAND," HE SAID, "WILL PROTECT A BRITISH SUBJECT IN WHATEVER LAND HE MAY BE."

That was in 1850.

✦ ✦ ✦

Once upon a time Germany despatched a gunboat to Agadir harbour to "protect German interests," and to encourage France to grant her concessions in Africa.

Seventy-nine words spoken by a British statesman at a public banquet brought that gunboat scurrying back, and referred a peaceful settlement.

There was nothing made about Mr. Lloyd George's seventy-nine words. Only a few sincerely. Only Germany's realisation that he meant what he said.

"If a situation were to be forced upon us in which peace could only be preserved by the surrender of the great and beneficent position Britain has won by centuries of heroism and achievement, by allowing Britain to be treated where her interests were vitally affected as if she were of no account in the Cabinet of nations, then I say emphatically that peace at that price would be a humiliation intolerable for a great country like ours to endure."

The Guildhall speech of Lloyd George sounded much like another Ministerial platitude. In reality it was a thunder-clap that electrified the Chancelleries of Europe.

That was in July, 1911.

TO-DAY THE SPEECHES OF OUR POLITICIANS SOUND LIKE THUNDERCLAPS—BUT IN REALITY ARE MERELY PLATITUDES.

A Saga of Inertia

"Once upon a time . . ."

That is how we have to tell of the power and glory of Britain in 1938.

"Once upon a time . . ."

Those words will be our epitaph unless the challenges of Palmerston and Lloyd George are to echo again.

FOR THE HISTORY OF ENGLAND NOW IS STEEPED IN SHAME AND COWARDICE.

OUR POWER AND GLORY ARE HELD IN CONTEMPT.

OUR FLAG IS SNEERED AT.

Once upon a time the British lion sprang if you cut off an Englishman's ear, or injured a British subject's property, or launched a gunboat.

Now you can diddle Britain out of millions of pounds and seize her oil wells. You can even kill a score of Englishmen—

AND GET AWAY WITH IT!

We merely turn the other cheek, and pray that our falling prestige will be raised.

✦ ✦ ✦

EVEN TO BRAZIL WE TURNED THE OTHER CHEEK.

Dictator Vargas proclaimed a new constitution, cynically announced suspension of the payment of interest and asking funds.

Did the British Navy sail?

Did we demonstrate in the harbour of Rio de Janeiro?

Not on your life! All that happened was that the London Stock Exchange suspended all dealing in Brazilian Government and municipal securities.

When Vargas's move was first rumoured, our Foreign Secretary said that it was hoped that the Brazilian Government would take no action pending negotiations.

Brazil took no notice.

"H.M. Government," said the Foreign Secretary, "have under serious consideration the new situation which has thus arisen."

Brazil took no notice.

"H.M. representative," said the Foreign Secretary, "has been instructed to urge the Brazilian Government to reconsider

the matter in view of the deplorable effect that that action created in this country."

Brazil still took no notice.

And though there is £207,000,000 of British capital in Brazil, the incident presumably is closed.

✦ ✦ ✦

EVEN TO MEXICO, TOO, THE LION OF BRITAIN TURNED THE OTHER CHEEK.

Mexico's Government expropriated British-owned oil wells valued at £40,000,000. Declines to pay any interest on her loans. Treats Great Britain with contempt.

What happened?

In as wrath the British Government sends a rude little note. There's talk too of the big oil companies boycotting Mexican oil and thereby compelling the Mexicans to give them back their wells.

But it is unlikely that the British Government will play any part, even the powerful Sinclairs, whom Mexico has robbed, have failed to stir the courage of our Cabinet.

NEITHER FOR THE PRIDE OF ITS POOR NOR FOR THE GOLD OF ITS RICH WILL THE BRITISH LION NOW LEAP AND CRUSH ITS ENEMIES.

By Charles Wilberforce

To Franco's suffering Spain we have also turned our smarting "other cheek" for month after month.

He sinks our ships. He massacres our seamen. He plays as much hell as he pleases—and gets away with it.

Read, if you can stand it, this story of our shame. And ask yourself then why the whole world says we're yellow.

Read this tale of "The Retail General and the Greatest Empire"—and blush to the roots of your hair.

✦ ✦ ✦

In April, 1937 . . . Mr. Baldwin's heroics.

"Britain," he said, "will not tolerate interference with our shipping."

In August, 1937 . . . Mr. Eden's hysterics.

"Britain," he said, "reserves the right to take such action as the occasion demands, on the event of further attacks."

BY SEPTEMBER FRANCO HAD RECEIVED A POSITIVE FAN-MAIL. SIX NOTES FROM OUR GOVERNMENT.

SIX NOTES—NOT ONE REPLY.

Five months go by and another British vessel kisses the bottom of the sea. And Mr. Eden's pen . . . still, he thinks, more mighty than the sword and cuts it to ribbons their again. "Our patience," he wrote, "is not inexhaustible."

Singularly worded, said the newspapers.

"O STING," I JOTTED IN MY DIARY. "O STING, WHERE IS THY DEATH?"

For the British lion that purrs, to spring so fearfully in February, sank back on its haunches and yawned in magnanimous May.

On May 11th:

"The British Agent at Burgos has been asked to make a strong protest against the unwarrantable bombing of British ships on May 9th."

On May 24th Mr. R. A. Butler announces in the House that no reply has been received.

"After considering those incidents—sinkings and deaths—the Government has been forced to conclude either that deliberate attacks are being made on British ships or that these are being dropped hit-and-miss."

On May 31st Mr. Butler announces in the House that no reply has been received.

After having "protested" on May 11th and "taking the matter further" on May 24th, Sir Robert Hodgson was forced to undergo the additional humiliation of "impressing upon the Burgos authorities the 'serious view'" that Britain took on May 31st.

And the Premier, too, put his oath in. Reluctant to defend our own ships, he had no hesitation in tut-tutting the maiming and death of Spain's defenceless citizens.

ANOTHER THUNDERCLAP?

YES . . . ANOTHER THUNDERCLAP WHICH EUROPE SNEERINGLY BURIED AS A PLATITUDE.

Two days later—the war of words went on. And Britain, terrified to fire a projectile, was hesitated to explode a new phrase.

Another ship goes down. Another strong protest goes up.

It is announced that "the Cabinet has decided it will no longer stand by while so-and-so and so-and-so."

The result?

Franco impudently speaks at last.

"We regret the damage done," he said.

THE DAMAGE DONE!

NEITHER THIS GENERATION NOR THE GENERATION AFTER WILL BE ABLE TO CALCULATE ONE-MILLIONTH OF THE DAMAGE DONE IF THE BRITISH LION LIES LOW AND COWERS ANY LONGER.

When the Spanish Government planes bombed a German battleship Hitler sent his warships to Almeria and bombarded dock with 200 shells—finding fire all time attacks by upon on German ships.

That's what Hitler did. Swiftly. And surely.

Is Franco to get away with a gibe that he will get guarantee as safety of OUR ships?

Purge—two of them have been smashed by the bombers. And in return we posted large-nose letters pistols reach the Britisher that talk has materialised into deeds.

It was the fawning merchant service which bombed day see poker in the Mediterranean—long before the Navy followed them in Sicilian lanes that the Navy goes to protect them now.

Think, ladies and gentlemen, of Robert Walpole and Jenkins's ear. Think of Palmerston and the Jew in Athens.

THINK OF A DOZEN SUCH STATESMEN AND A HUNDRED SUCH SITUATIONS—AND ASK YOURSELF AGAIN WHY THE WORLD THINKS WE'RE YELLOW IN 1938!

✦ ✦ ✦

Arms are merely tools to implement a policy, said the Sunday Pictorial of the 8th of May. And the trouble is that Britain has no policy at all.

That's still the miserable position in many spheres to-day. We're getting on with our rearmaments like wildfire. And we're talking about it till we're blue in the face.

But it's not only the guns that count. It's the MEN in them —and the MEN BEHIND THEM.

Brazil, Mexico. And now Franco's Spain.

Europe is watching our sluggish impotence in these affairs. They are no longer judging us by the speed with which we are producing our weapons; they are judging us by our cowardice in using them.

Hitler is judging us. Hitler, whose ships bombarded Almeria because Spain bombed ONE of his vessels.

Mussolini, too. And France. And Russia.

And this is the verdict they are delivering in the secrecy of their Cabinets. This is why they are contemptuous of our muscular Navy and our growing Air Force.

"YOU CAN STEAL BRITISH PROPERTY—AND GET AWAY WITH IT."

"YOU CAN SINK BRITISH SHIPS—AND GET AWAY WITH IT."

"YOU CAN EVEN KILL BRITISH SAILORS—AND GET AWAY WITH THAT, TOO."

That's what the world is saying. That's why the world is sneering at our power and glory and deriding our flag.

Isn't This Our Duty?

I say that the pride of the nation, with the most powerful Navy, has been humbled too long.

I say that the people of Britain are sick of their shame, that they demand to hold their heads high again.

There are dark days ahead in Europe. Any fool knows that. And the people are asking what will be the future of a Britain that tolerates the death of Bruni and the murder of Mexico, and stands for months after murder at the hands of a rebel?

What a time for Englishmen is must be!—if Hitler, Mussolini, and the Japs had the jitters over US occasionally.

No one wants to fire one gun all over the globe. No one wants to be rushed headlong into an affair for the sake of a battle.

But remember Lloyd George's speech in the Guildhall on the evening of July twenty-seven years ago.

Our Government can still repeat it—

If Britain is to be treated where her interests are vitally affected as if she is of no account in the Cabinet of Nations, if intolerable humiliation by the price which Britain has to pay for peace—

THEN EVERY MAN AND WOMAN IN THE LAND WILL STAND BEHIND THE GOVERNMENT IN ANY MOVE IT DECIDES TO MAKE. EVERY MAN WILL KNOW—AND DO—HIS DUTY.

✦ ✦ ✦

The world is saying that the colour of the British flag is yellow.

The world must learn that the colours of that flag are Red, White and Blue.

They are calling us cowards!

The school ran to a tight schedule and we were kept busy throughout the day. The bell rang when action was needed: the wake up bell; the class bell; the refectory bell and so on. There was no dawdling. Punctuality was demanded. No pupil had a watch, since watches were unavailable for our age. Once you got into the routine, which in my case was from day one, you could tell the time of day. By the time the second bell rang, five minutes later, you had to be seated in class. Grandfather clocks were located around the school and all kept perfect time.

Our weekly letters home were written on Sunday morning. We were helped in its composition, by looking at the blackboard, where the week's events, had been chalked on. All boys had to write home, and prior to posting, many were read by a second party prior to sealing the envelope.

Outdoor games varied per season—rugger at Christmas and Easter terms though much depended on the weather. Up north it was bitterly cold at Easter and many events were cancelled due to frost or snow. When snow fell, snowball fights occurred, but were discouraged. Tobogganing was another favourite pastime.

Boredom was never an issue, as we were kept busy throughout the day. I was in a Catholic Preparatory School and Mass was a daily event. Religious classes occurred throughout the week, and prior to the beginning of class, prayers were said and again before and after meals. The words A.M.D.G. (Ad Majorem dei Gloriam) headed our written subject and L.D.S. (Laus Deus Semper) ended our paper. In this Catholic school, we were being trained to be future leaders and were expected to lead in our religious beliefs.

I was not at Hodder for pleasure. I was there to improve my academia. In my first term, I was placed in Preparatory, its lowest class: average age 9 years. I was 10. Some of the boys were 7 and 8 and all were well ahead of me academically. I was two to three years behind. In the end of term examination, I was placed 11 out of 14 and as a result earned another term in Preparatory. In the subjects taught by Ernest Britto (D 1), I performed well. I had a lot to catch up with, for I had not touched on many subjects required: no Catechism, Scripture, French, History, Geography and the ten subtitles of Preparatory English. I was therefore trailing in class, even though I was the oldest. Fortunately Miss Cowley, the only female teacher at Hodder, encouraged me, with gentleness and persuasion. By the end of my second term, I came eighth with distinction. But the only distinction that was visible was that I was nearly 11 years of age in a class averaging 9. From then on, I improved rapidly, for I had one term in Lower Elements and another in Upper Elements before World War II broke out on 3 September 1939. Academia now took second place to age in my class advancement.

Our best day was Sunday, for on that day Willie visited us from Stonyhurst. He spent the allowed time with us, which was one hour exactly. His pockets bulged with 'tuck', and this had to be eaten before we retuned into the building. No problem! We were allowed sixpence of pocket money per week, which was handed during Wednesday's lunch time. We were allowed to keep 30 shillings in the Rector's safe, and any amount demanded had to be signed for. Unlike the bank, a good reason had to be given for withdrawals and with a permitted maximum of two shillings.

As long as you worked hard and abided by the rules and routines, school was enjoyable. If you decided to go wayward a 'Ferula' helped you to return back to 'sanity' and discipline. My main problem was that I shouted too much, but this could be medically attributed to my mother's and aunts' deafness, as the three suffered from Otosclerosis. Conversations at home were loud. Raised voices were discouraged at Hodder. Once you learned the school routines, the only changes that took place were in the classes; from Preparatory to Figures: from Class 1 to Class 4.

Returning Home

At end of term, we travelled to Euston Station where we were invariably met by my Great Uncle Ernest. We spent a few days in London, before boarding the liner at either Tilbury or Southampton en route to Gibraltar. All liners serving the Empire called at Gibraltar, and the best for comfort and food were the P & O Strathclass: Stratheden, Strathallen, Strathnaver and Strathmore. All experienced the same challenges when steaming though the Bay of Biscay: pitching, rolling, empty dining rooms and decks.

Czechoslovakia

Bar Easter, which was too short in vacation time to merit a Gibraltar trip, Willie, Great Uncle Ernest or others took the arduous job of caring for us on board. In my second term at Christmas, we were accompanied by my mother and Lennie on the Orient Liner 'Oriana', which left Gibraltar on 18 September 1938. Both accompanied us to Stonyhurst and stayed at the Shireburn Arms in Hurst Green (M 8). The reason on this occasion (unknown to me) was the international crisis, when war with Germany was imminent over Czechoslovakia. My father wrote: 'On 28 September 1938, the international situation having grown worse, mummy and Lennie proceeded to the Shireburn Arms for refuge. On the same day Mr Neville Chamberlain, Prime Minister proceeded for the third time to Germany by air and succeeded in arriving at a settlement in Munich, which averted a war.' Three days before we left for England, on 15 September 1938, Premier Chamberlain flew to Germany. Preparations for war were advancing locally. A.R.P. (Air Raid Precaution) shelters (I 3) and the early stages of building an airport (D 10). London was readying itself to evacuate two million people. The majority of the U.K. male population supported Churchill and Eden. Both wanted Chamberlain to defy Hitler. Most women on the other hand preferred appeasement and supported Chamberlain's stance.

Germany annexed Austria in the spring of 1938. Now it was the turn of the Czechs to surrender the Sudetenland by 2.30 p.m. on 30 September 1938. Chamberlain persuaded them to do precisely that. The next day, following his meeting with Hitler in Munich, Chamberlain returned to Britain. As he left the aircraft he waved a piece of paper, 'I believe it is peace for our time.'

As my father could not return to Gibraltar during the 1914-18 war, he wanted to ensure that if the same happened to us, my mother and sister would be close by. When the clouds of war had blown over, albeit on a temporary basis, they boarded the liner Orion and returned to Gibraltar on 8 October 1938, after a rather unpleasant trip.

At Hodder, rules were made and never stretched, but during the 1938 Munich Crisis, for once, they were. My mother's persuasive and persistent requests, to the point of sobbing, were too much for the Rector to bear. He allowed the unthinkable. On two occasions we were permitted to go out for high tea, to the Shireburn Arms.

The reason given why exeats were discouraged, was simply that it upset the boys on their return. These exeats were never to be repeated again, except on one other occasion. As President of the Mediterranean Racing Club, my father had been invited to watch the Grand National at Aintree, when 'Workman' won. A surprise visit to us was naturally on the cards and an exeat arranged for that Sunday (K 3). I always looked forward to the day when this would happen on a regular basis. That day never came.

Returning Home

All the sporting pleasures, both indoor and outdoor, were available at Hodder, but the terms lasted far too long. The thrill and pleasure of seeing the top of the Rock from the liner at Tarifa and then an hour later seeing my parents on board the 'Marie Claire' was beyond any rational explanation. It was joy in its purest form.

To return to Gib was a wonderful experience. A mother and father who could not be bettered. Aunt Kittita who lived and cared for us, with Uncle Tuto and Aunt Mema in support, plus my grandparents and everyone else. Excellent cuisine and freedom to roam with my friends, anywhere. Hodder bore no comparison with home. I could not understand my school friends when they spoke of the food at Hodder being good. I often felt like telling them to come home and taste ours. But this would not have gone down well.

One aspect of my schooling that made its mark on all of us as children, and later on as adults, was our appreciation of home, especially when we compared with those of our friends, who remained behind. We also acquired that travel confidence at a very early age that usually only seasoned travellers have.

When the holiday ended and we had to go back to school, tears flowed profusely at home in Secretary's Lane, and my father and Papa Willie were the only ones to accompany us to the liners. The Flower brothers always ensured our departures went smoothly. As the propellers started up; the ship began vibrating and Gibraltar gradually disappeared under the Tarifa Hills, we knew we would not see our parents for another long three months.

Back in London, Great Uncle Ernest (K 8) would be there to guide us back to the school train. If we had a few days to spare, he would leave us at the Gaumont or Odeon Cinema in Marble Arch. There he would buy us our cinema tickets and sit us in the front row. 'Mam' he would say to the usherette, 'keep an eye on these boys until I return'. Sometimes he would be late from his court sittings, and we would see the film twice.

In 1938, Christmas Day was spent on board the P.O. liner Stratheden. Term had ended too late for us to make home on time. We spent the day accompanied by great Uncle Ernest. He was a kind and generous uncle, and many of his actions remain vivid in my mind. One such was when crossing London's Oxford Street. Without notice, his walking stick struck me right across the chest. I was about to dash across the street, not having seen the traffic coming. 'Cecil', he said, 'London is not Gibraltar. You cross at the traffic lights and you look both ways'. I always took his advice onboard.

London, Easter 1939

At Easter 1939, Lennie was accepted to Farnborough Hillside Convent, and as we could not return to Gibraltar, due to the short vacations, London once again became our venue for entertainment.

The Stagnettos once again accompanied us. With a father who enjoyed all aspects of London life and a mother who loved the shops, we had the best of parents. We always stayed at different hotels in London. We went greyhound racing at the White City; saw Madam Tussuads; London's museums; Hampton Court; the Tower of London; skated at Westminster ice-rink; swam at Dolphin Square; boating on the Serpentine and enjoyed a car ride to Windsor Castle and Eton College. We attended mass at Farm Street, the Brompton Oratory and Westminster Cathedral. And at night ventured out to several of its theatres and cinemas. We toured London on double deckers, so by the time we left, we were quite familiar with Central London. The game of Monopoly also helped.

On my return to Hodder, I was placed in Upper Elements, having been in Lower Elements one term. It was obvious to me, that at this rate, I would be in Figures by Christmas, and hopefully, I would be one year in a class with my own age group. This did not happen as war broke out on 3 September 1939, and my return to Hodder was rendered impossible.

Summer Holiday 1939

Summer holidays in 1939 were no different for me than the year before. We could not go to Spain. There were many problems that had not been solved by the Franco regime, and which could affect any individual, who dared to cross (D 14) its devastated country. But we had a racecourse and plenty of green land for recreation. The races were always enjoyable and my favourite horses that I invariably backed, had English connections: Staines, Cynthia Green, Royal Oak, Rex and Bolero (E 5).

Behind the scenes, yet openly visible to the civilian population, deep underground shelters (I 3) began to be built, under the Governorship of General Ironside (I 4). They were called A.R.P. (Air Raid Precaution) shelters and were designed to protect 15,000 civilians at a cost of £100,000. The 1,000 wives and children of the Gibraltar Garrison, would in an emergency, be sent back to the United Kingdom. The Governor was quoted as saying: 'We plan to adopt the rabbit-in-burrow system in war-time, when residents will never be far beyond the entrance to the shelters'. They were strong enough to withstand 'a direct hit by a two ton bomb and were 100 percent safe'.

I knew the clouds of war were close, for my mother's ears were constantly glued to the radio. She was an avid listener and invariably tuned to the BBC World Service at night. There was too much radio crackling in the daytime. Spanish news could be easily heard, but was unreliable and not to be trusted. There was no change in the number of British warships (H 12) calling here. Yet war was only round the corner. Main Street was always packed with servicemen, and the honky tonks always full with inebriated sailors. But if you wanted to read the international press, mainly English, you could buy your papers from Sacrarello's Newsagents albeit, seven or eight days after publication. By then it was not news, but half a loaf is better than none.

War

On Sunday 3 September 1939 at 11 a.m. Britain and France declared that they were at war with Germany. Returning from mass, we met Fred Sacarello, who predicted that war would last six years. He was proven correct. Little changed in our routines, except that we were made fully aware where the A.R.P. shelters were, and how to use them in an emergency. There was little chance of an attack here, for the Royal Navy ruled the waves and German planes could not fly this distance. I witnessed within weeks, two anti-submarine nets laid across the Admiralty Harbour entrance and with considerable sadness, the end of horse racing at North Front, and its replacement by a runway (D 10). Victoria Gardens, its greenery and other beauty spots were replaced by stones, concrete and tar. Locally most agreed, that Hitler's reign would be short lived, perhaps a few months or at most two years.

HODDER. LONGRIDGE.

K.

Hodder Place.

Upper Elements.

Clitheroe. Father with three sons. *(1939).*

Hodder River. Father Belton S.J. with life saving equipment.

Mother with Stagnettos *(1938).*

The war effort *(1942).*

HODDER. LONGRIDGE.

K.

Christmas Day with great-uncle Ernest. S.S. Stratheden *(1938)*.

Post Office stamp. S.S. Ranpura. Gibraltar, the travel key of the Mediterranean.

Frank Forster, Spitfire pilot with his newly-wed wife Eileen. *(1946)*.

Ration Book *(1940)*.

Identity Card *(1940)*.

Christmas *(1940)*. Bitterly cold.

Cause of our M.I.5 visit. Note U.S.S.R. Flag *(1940)*.

HODDER. LONGRIDGE.

K.

Family in exile. Preston *(1943)*.

Paddy with Mrs. Wallbank. Longridge *(1942)*.

TO THE REFUGEES FROM GIBRALTAR

Your fellow-countrymen in the United Kingdom offer you shelter in hostels in London. In return, they are confident, you will do what you can to make as light as possible the task of providing you with food and shelter in a country at war. We must ask you therefore to do your part by keeping the hostel clean and your own rooms tidy, and also to help in the preparation and distribution of food.

In each hostel there will be a Commandant, responsible to the Government, who will be in charge. He will show you what has to be done and will ask you to appoint leaders who will help both him and yourselves in the running of the hostel. Good organisation will help us to make you comfortable; disorder can only prolong the discomforts that you have already suffered for the sake of your country.

In the interests of your own health and of the health of your hosts, you are asked not to go outside the hostel until you have been examined by the appointed medical officer. Medical treatment will be provided for those who need it.

When the medical examination has been completed and you are at liberty to leave the hostel, take care that you know how to find your way back. We ask you also to return to the hostel early in the evening and in no case later than the appointed hour of closing, which for the present will be 10.0 in the evening.

It is important for your safety, and for the safety of your companions and hosts, that you should take the greatest care to cover the windows of your rooms, from dusk to daylight, so that no light is seen from outside.

In each hostel, a list of the guests will be prepared as soon as possible, and when these have all been completed we shall be able to help you to find friends from whom you have been separated on the journey.

MINISTRY OF HEALTH,
Whitehall, London, S.W.1.
August, 1940.

They were not refugees but evacuees:
a subtle difference.

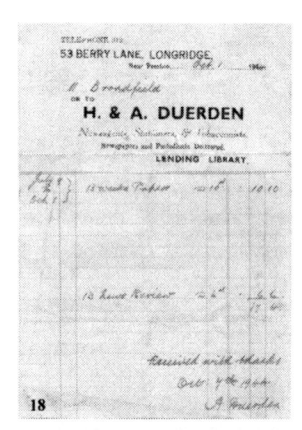

H&A.
Duerden.
Excellent service
(1944).

Broadfield. Longridge.
Post *(1945)*.

Progress in my studies was now to be further downgraded. The Governor let it be known, that until a convoy system was operational, it would be unwise for students or teachers to leave by sea. With my Christmas term at Hodder beginning in two weeks time, it was obvious that we would not be travelling to the U.K. for some time. To this end, the good Admiral offered the use of his ballroom as a temporary classroom. Many of the U.K. teachers accepted his offer. I and many others spent our Christmas term at 'The Mount'. As war progressed, our school venue changed once again, this time to Wellesley Hall. Michael Brufal's aunt, Jackie Yule, could not return to her teaching post in Malta, for the same reason and became one of our teachers. To teach different age groups, in different streams and subjects and in one large classroom, must have been particularly difficult for the teachers. There was a war on, even though 'all was quiet on the Gibraltar front'. (D 14)

Despite the war, life went on as usual. Fishing, cycling, walking, picnics and all that a schoolboy enjoys. Germany was too far way to be of any consequence. With no convoys in sight, we continued enjoying our enforced holiday. At the end of the Easter term 1940, I partook in the school's end of term play: 'The Rose and the Ring'. (D11, D12). Sixteen years later, to the day I was to marry 'The Ring and the Rose': Ringrose.

Gibraltarians were 100 per cent with Britain, but the Gibraltar Chronicle of the day was still in colonial-baiting mood. Priority on our pavements was for the serving officers; and the natives, be they men or women, had to step off the pavements and onto our narrow streets. It was the courtesy demanded from all civilians for the King's uniform or badge, but by 1939, was on the wane, as a result of local political pressure. A misguided chronicler now resuscitated an event of the past.

This colonial insult could not be left without comment. In keeping with my father's political approach, he wrote an open letter to 'El Anunciador' newspaper. 'With the Gibraltar Chronicle refusing to give a full and unqualified apology to the people of Gibraltar for the insult offered to them, I deem it my duty to publish the full facts for the information of the public and particularly the government'. (L4, L5).

Gibraltarians were fully with Britain and our war effort was geared to that end. Some days before we left for England, the Loreto Covent pupils held their last concert at the Assembly Rooms. It ended gloriously, as in the 'Last Night of the Proms': 'Rule Britannia', 'Land of Hope and Glory' and other nationalistic songs, rang out through the night.

Madrid, Paris, London 1940

I was never able to read the unqualified apology expected from the Chronicle, for war events moved too fast. On 15 April 1940 I left for England by car, with my father, Willie and Peter: destination Stonyhurst. We were chauffeur driven in P.G. Russo's car: a very good, family friend. Special permission was obtained from Madrid's highest authority, without which we could not cross into, through and out of Spain. All our travelling papers bore that official Madrid stamp.

After the Civil War, Spain was a devastated country. The nation was destroyed, poverty rampant. Begging children in tattered and dirty clothes; with unwashed bodies and faces, and signs of malnutrition were everywhere to be seen. Our first stop was Malaga, where destruction was considerable. There we lunched and refuelled and then proceeded northwards through Granada and to our first night's resting place at the Albergue of Bailen. The Guardia Civil and the grey uniform police were everywhere to be seen. The main roads to the north were narrow and free from traffic. This allowed us to speed up. We were warned not to travel by night because of 'bandidos'. It was dangerous to stop in areas where trees predominated or where walls formed part of the landscape. We broke our journey only in areas where the vision was unobstructed and no humans could be seen on the horizon. So when one of us needed to go to the toilet, we had to wait, irrespective of the urgency, sometimes an hour or longer. When we did stop, we all had to 'pee' at the same time, standing in a circle, facing out, each keeping his eye on his respective visual fields. There were no petrol stations on the highway and refuelling was done in the towns where we stopped for meals. You could count the number of cars on the road between towns on the fingers of one hand.

There was not one town we saw which had not been severely damaged. Travelling by night was verboten, so we rose early to make the best of the light. Lunch and refuelling in Madrid was hair-raising, for everywhere we went, faces of hunger, defeat and hate approached us begging. When we arrived at the Christina Hotel in San Sebastian, we were totally exhausted, it being late evening. Despite the poverty and beggars seen from our rooms, the hotel functioned normally, as if nothing had happened since 1936.

The next morning, we drove to the Irun-Hendaye border, where Spanish officials checked our documents over and over. They insisted on calling Madrid, to double check the veracity of our permits. Eventually and many nerve wracking hours later, we were cleared. 'After considerable difficulty,' wrote my father 'we crossed the frontier and proceeded by taxi to Biarritz, where we spent the day'. As our chauffeur and car were refused permission to exit Spain and had to return to Gibraltar, we engaged two Spanish porters. Halfway across the neutral ground bridge they stopped and their French counterparts now trolleyed the three large school trunks towards their frontier post. There was no evidence of war preparations in Biarritz or its surrounding areas. That night, we caught the Biarritz (Hendaye) train to Paris and arrived next morning, after a comfortable night rest in our wagon-lits. A good lunch at Le Bourget airport, before boarding our plane to Heston airport, made our air trip worthwhile. Before boarding the Air France flight, we were warned not to touch the planes gear under the port holes (wires on the side of the plane) and not to put our fingers through the fuselage. (Metal planes were not yet in use). I thought I saw a German plane some miles away, but it never approached us. The war was still in its early and relatively civilised stage.

My father wrote, '... at 3.30 p.m. left by Air France for London, and arrived at Heston 5.15 p.m., and at the Winston Hotel in Jermyn St at 6.00 p.m.' No photographs were taken in Spain, as it was illegal for transit tourists to carry cameras. The London we arrived in was now one of wartime and the blackout made walking hazardous for all. One good meal, early to bed and the L.M.S. train to Preston, 36 hours later. On this occasion we were accompanied by my father, as school had started some days earlier. He returned to London immediately and now his only way home was by air. He wrote 'left London 1 May for Paris, on 2 for Marseilles and on 3 for Tangier, crossing by ferry boat to Gibraltar on 5 May 1940'.

'Soon after, the evacuation of women and children was ordered and mummy with Lennie left Gibraltar by the Orient Liner S.S. Ormonde arriving in England on 22 May after a very unpleasant journey'. What should have been four days was now eight due to the Ormonde having to zig-zag in convoy. The bad weather, seasickness, boat drills, life jackets having to be permanently on, the fear of being torpedoed could not have made their journey pleasant. The only plus was that they had not been torpedoed. The mental strain that my mother must have suffered was considerable; her husband, sisters and others left behind; the sea trip in dangerous waters; and no news from her three sons at Stonyhurst, as a result of war and censorship.

On 10 May the German army broke through into Holland and within five days the Dutch had surrendered. The German army then proceeded southwards into Belgium to outflank the French army holding the Maginot line. Brussels surrendered on 17 May. By 26 May the evacuation of the British army was in full swing, and by 2 June, the German army was in full control of Dunkirk. A Stonyhurst old boy was awarded the first Victoria Cross of the war: Major Ervine Andrews for his valour at Dunkirk (M 5).

We had lost contact with our parents, but not for long, for shortly after their arriving in England, my mother and Lennie sped north and lodged at the Shireburn Arms. Neither of us had heard from the other for six weeks, and though it was difficult for us to see her, her persuasive and tearful ways once again, won the day with Father Belton, S.J.

With our summer holidays about to begin and nowhere to go, Willie and my mother identified and rented a two-month holiday home at Bowness-on-Windemere. Glebe House was to be our temporary home. We had a putting green right across the road; boats for hire 100metres away and an ice cream vendor within yards. The creamy ice creams were delicious, the best I ever tasted.

News from Gibraltar was non-existent, but fortunately one of my mother's letters reached my father just in time. Our extended family of Aunt Kittita, Uncle Tuto, Aunt Mema and daughter Paddy were in Gibraltar, when French aircraft, now allied to Germany, released their heavy bomb load on our town. One large bomb remained silent in our garden. It was seen by my father a few days later, and eventually removed by the bomb disposal squad (L 7)

Our extended family were in Gibraltar on the nights of 25 and 26 July, on board the 'Ulster Monarch'. The ship had sailed to Casablanca, but as the Vichy Government of France now took orders from Berlin, consent to land the evacuees in Casablanca was refused. The Casablanca experience and the conditions onboard were bad enough, war or no war, for any reasonable person to bear. The ship returned to Gibraltar. Permission to land here was militarily refused, and shortly after the ship sailed for Tilbury, London. From there, my family were taken to Dr Barnardo's home in Barkingside, Essex. Its previous residents had been evacuated to a safer area. They now had a bird's eye view of the Battle of Britain, but not for long. Uncle Tuto knew our address, but because of censorship it took him four days to obtain our telephone number. Once contact was made, they proceeded northwards. Not one looked well on arrival. Paddy had a generalised skin infection, consistent with the bad conditions experienced on board. For all of us the reunion on that wonderful day was one of the best ever experienced.

The Battle of Britain was now in full swing. We were winning the air war. I became an avid reader of the Daily Express. Comics were out for good. The holiday at Bowness came sadly to an end, far too quickly. There, we were restricted from going further than one mile from home, and if we rowed on the lake, no further than a small island half a mile from the promenade, just in case a German fighter swooped down and gunned us. It had been done in France. No one questioned whether such planes had the fuel to reach the north. Swimming in the lake was out; too cold, no buoyancy and fear of a German Messerschmitt. Much of our time was spent on the putting green.

IN ABSENTIA (1938-1956)

L.
Selected articles written by BECCLES (Albert Isola) in EL ANNUNCIADOR.

Unity is Strength

The Chamber of Commerce has acted promptly. The Board of Directors are meeting tomorrow at 5-30 p.m. and an invitation to attend has been issued to all those interested in the draft Ordinance prohibiting the citizens of this city from trading without a licence.

Everyone without exception is interested in the proposed legislation. If it does not at the moment affect some of us, it may do so at a later date or it may affect our children in the future. The Government intend to take away from us, not as an emergency measure, the right which from time immemorial citizens of this town have enjoyed, a right to choose their own means of livelihood by carrying on such a trade as may appeal to them. If legislation of this nature is passed, the time will come when the Licensing Authority will decide in what particular manner we must earn our living. There are nations where the Head of the State decides how individuals must be brought up and in what particular way they shall serve the State. The policy of the British Empire is contrary to this, and no one need doubt that if there is unity among us and strong representations are made to the authorities, and to the Colonial Office, if necessary, the Ordinance contemplated cannot pass in its present form.

We therefore appeal to all citizens to attend the meeting. Let us forget who discovered the Government's intentions as expressed in the Ordinance and how it came to our knowledge, this has not the slightest importance. If it had not come to our knowledge, it would have been made known sooner or later in some other form. Let us attend the meeting, let us listen to those who can explain the proposed legislation and above all let us limit our discussions to the fundamental point at issue. There are included many clauses in the Ordinance which when, carefully read, will be objected to. But the time to make these objections is not at this particular meeting, when its sole object should be the maintenance of our right to trade. When the Government acknowledges such a right, representations on other clauses as well as on the taxes suggested can be made.

We know that Mr. Peter G. Russo, O.B.E., J.P., (Chairman of the City Council) and other Councillors will attend the meeting. Let us hope that the unofficial members of the Executive Council will also attend, even if only to acquaint the Government of the attitude of the meeting towards the proposed Ordinance and the nature of the discussions. We ask all members of the Legal Profession to attend, they can be of immense service to the cause.

Let everyone attending the meeting understand that no one is interested in the actual speaker but in what he says. Those who cannot command the English language need have no fear of speaking at the meeting, they will be well understood. We feel sure that the Chairman will permit those who are better able to do so to address the meeting in the Spanish language.

The issue is a matter of life or death to us. It merits far more attention than the words uttered by General Hunter in 1919. Unity is strength, it was then, and it is so today.

El Anunciador *(5/12/39)*
War broke out on 3rd September 1939.

"The issue is a matter of life or death to us!".

MEN OF GOODWILL

The announcement in the Press that His Excellency the Governor has acceded to address the citizens of this town at midnight on New Year's Eve and thus re-establish a custom which existed for many years, has been received with great satisfaction. That it is the wish of the people, there cannot be the slightest doubt. That His Excellency is put to a certain amount of inconvenience, can well be understood. The occasion has no political significance. The assembling at Government House is an expression of our loyalty and devotion to His Majesty and of our implicit confidence in his representative. In fact, it is a desire to meet our Governor and a wish that he be allowed the opportunity of meeting his people. Advantage of the occasion is taken to wish His Excellency and Lady Liddell the very best wishes for a prosperous New Year.

The people of Gibraltar hope that the New Year will bring some better form of understanding and goodwill between them and those in responsible positions. They are today far from satisfied. Many of their complaints are justified. These can hardly be called problems, for solutions are easy. Incompetence on the part of some officials may be at the root, but lack of a desire to treat us as Britishers is very prevalent.

His Excellency can count on the support of the whole colony as long as the rights and liberties of its citizens are preserved and equal treatment with other British subjects is meted out. It is our earnest wish to collaborate and to give every assistance in our power.

We look forward with interest to His Excellency's address, which will be welcomed as coming from a man who in such short a time has gained the confidence of the people.

El Anunciador (29/12/39).

EVERYBODY'S BUSINESS L.

The people of Gibraltar are of a generous and charitable disposition. There is hardly any appeal for funds in aid of some charitable object that is not responded to with absolute generosity. I would not dare to mention all the charitable institutions for fear of leaving out some particular one which is as worthy of mention as the others. There are also many ladies and gentlemen who give their time and attention to the needs of the poor, and who take pains to see that their needs are satisfied. But there are too many poor in Gibraltar, and sometimes one feels that there are too many calls on the private purse, and some other means should be found to ameliorate their sufferings and above all to make them self-supporting. We need official action to put this matter right, to enforce a living wage for the working classes, to assist the aged by means of old age pensions, to help the unemployed to live, and above all to supply decent houses to live in. This need is becoming greater every day.

Here is a problem which must be solved and which is so urgent that it calls for no other solution at the moment than an inmediate appeal to the generosity of the people.

There are about 2,000 children attending Government aided schools. The Education Ordinance imposes a penalty on parents who fail to provide elementary education for their children. A school attendance officer has the responsibility of seeing that children attend school daily. The only lawful excuses for their absence are sickness or "unavoidable cause". The consequent result of continued absence is that the child misses the lessons that are taught on such days, loses interest and fails to keep up with his class.

I have been able to ascertain that many children cannot go to school for an "unavoidable cause". They have no boots. If they happen to have a pair, these are of no use in rainy weather. Usually such consist of rubber shoes (plimsoles) because they are cheaper; and with wear, holes appear. I am not passing on information, I have actually spoken to some parents, seen the shoes and ascertained the reasons why their children cannot be properly, if at all, so provided. Poverty is at the root of it. I could hardly believe my own eyes. Another "unavoidable cause" is lack of clothes, particularly overcoats or some protection against rain and cold.

I made a series of visits last Thursday. It was pouring and I was able to gather the required information. My first visit was to "Nectar", a large store with cubicles where whole families live together, situate behind some houses opposite the Cricket Ground in North Front. I am not going to describe the place, because no description could meet the purpose. There are 32 children living in the place and with a few exceptions, all are of school age. They must walk to a school in Lower Castle Road daily.

L.

In a cubicle, a cabdriver his wife and seven children live. His little girl aged 11 did not go to school on Thursday last because she had to look after her mother who was sick in bed. Another child aged 9 set out to go to school and on reaching Bayside returned home due to the force of the wind. She had neither an overcoat nor raincoat and her dress, if rinsed, dripped with water. The other child of school age had a pair of rubber shoes with holes, she also had stayed at home. Other children had scarcely any clothes to wear and were being looked after by neighbours.

In another cubicle, a widow with five children lives. Two of them had been unable to go to school, for lack of shoes and clothes. An employee of a Corporation earning 31/-d per week lives in another cubicle with two children of school age, who had been unable to attend school. The same reason was given, I actually saw the shoes they were wearing, rubber shoes with holes in the soles. A coalheaver with wife and two children live in another cubicle, an unhealthy and damp place. These children had only pullovers and no coats or overcoats to wear. They also remained at home. In a house opposite "Nectar" 4 families live including fifteen children. Not one of these had been able to attend school. They were very poorly dressed and hardly able to leave the house in any kind of weather. I gathered from my visit to North Front that if these children were to receive education, they had to be supplied with boots, clothing and overcoats and that it was really necessary to engage some means of conveyance to take them to and from school. I was more than convinced that the parents did not earn enough to provide their children with theses necessities. I also called at a few houses in town. I purposely omit to publish the names of those I spoke to but give full addresses so that they can be identified. At No. 22 Willis' Road lives a mother with three children. She gets 14/- per week. She also receives assistance from the City Council. Two of her children of school age failed to attend because they had nothing to wear on their feet. The mother is saving up to buy clothing. I doubt if it is possible. At No. 49 Willis' Road House No. 41, a man, wife and five children reside. The earnings amount to 30/-d per week, and the rent is 13/6d per month. Three of their children being of school age were absentees for the same "unavoidable cause". At the same place but in House 37 a mother lives with her son and daughter on 12/-d per week. The son earns the money, her brother pays the rent, but the daughter was unable to go to school due to inability to buy shoes.

I could give you more examples still of the absolute necessity of providing shoes to children. At many places but particularly at No. 57, Willis' Road and No. 6 Lower Castle Road, some children were ill in bed due to colds undoubtedly caused through being ill-clad and shod. But if anyone is interested in preserving the future generation and in ascertaining for himself the deplorable conditions of childrens' clothing and footwear, I would invite him to go at 12-30 p.m. to the premises of that wonderful and praiseworthy institution "The Soup Kitchen" and see for himself.

I have asked myself what can be done about this whole matter. Perhaps it is hardly the time to call upon the Government to remedy this state of affairs. But it must be remedied and once again by those on whom so many calls are made. It is not a question of wanton neglect on the part of parents but of inability to supply the needs of their children. I am certain that the labourer with the present amount of his wages can hardly feed his family let alone clothe them. The education of his children must be a secondary consideration. Because education is compulsory, and children must leave their home for the purpose, it is essential that they should be c'othed. But parents cannot supply raincoats or overcoats or even proper footwear on 30/- a week. The problem is one which deserves our immediate attention. If we cannot help all those who require assistance, let us supply some.

Well to do parents are anxious to give their children a good education. They follow their mental progress with the same satisfaction as they follow their physical development and feel proud when scholarships and prizes are won. They look forward to the end of their children's carrier and even feel that their reward should be their children preparedness for live's strife. In fact, such parents can look forward to their children's prosperity. But the parents of the children living in the circumstances that I have described can give practically no attention to education. Not only must they depend on the Government to provide education for their children, but in the majority of cases, their wages are so low that they must depend on charitable institutions to assist them in their livelihood. If they lose their jobs they are completely helpless, and if they do not recieve assistance, they must starve. Laws exist in England to provide against such an eventuality, and only in exceptional circumstances must they depend on charity. The promulgation of similar legislation in Gibraltar is a matter difficult though not impossible to be tackled under present circumstances, but I sincerely hope that this can come under the Heading of Empire building. The Government can make it possible for parents to provide for their children without having recourse to charity. Pending any such solution let us solve it ourselves temporarily, render assistance to the Government, and at the same time ensure that children shall not absent themselves from school by the "unavoidable causes" of lacking clothing and footware. By not solving the question, we are just shirking our responsibility and our duty towards our own townsmen, risking that the future generation shall be an uneducated lot fit only for menial duties and permitting this Colony to have only an inferior complex as regards the Empire. The solution is to provide clothing and footwear for which purpose two things are necessary, funds and a Committee. As far as I can see, it is hardly possible to say what amount is required, but since my plan is to supply the needs, as when and according to the amounts recieved, the number of children in need will gradually diminish. Though it is the custom in Gibraltar to pass a list round when funds are required, on this occasion the appeal must be only to those who can not only afford but are willing to give. I am extremely anxious that none of us should be placed under any moral obligation to give in accordance with what others in the same conditions contribute or even to make any contribution. Let everyone decide for himself whether the cause commends itself to him, whether he can afford to give and above all whether he willingly desires to help.

At my repeated suggestions Miss Orosia Rugeroni of No. 216 Main Street, Gibraltar, has kindly consented temporarily to receive contributions, assist in forming a small Committee and immediately undertake to supply such clothing and footwear as may be necessary to those most in need. She will also make arrangements to provide a Charabanc for those children living in North Front to enable them to attend school in all weathers.

Acknowledgments will appear from time to time in the press as also the progress made by the Committee to serve this worthy cause.

El Anunciador. *6 de Febrero de 1940.*

El Anunciador *(1/3/40)*. L.

MEMO

TO THE EDITOR AND PUBLISHERS OF "THE GIBRALTAR CHRONICLE"

FROM BECCLES

Will you kindly publish a full and unqualified apology for the unwarranted insult to the people of Gibraltar contained in the verse under the heading "Street Manners" published last Wednesday or would you rather risk the consequences?

El Anunciador *(6/3/40)*. 4

EMPIRE-BREAKERS

By BECCLES

Since the Editor and Publishers of the "Gibraltar Chronicle" by their silence give the impression that they would rather ignore my demand for a full and unqualified apology to the people of Gibraltar for the insult offered to them, I deem it my duty to publish the full facts for the information of the public and particularly the Government.

On the 28th. February last the "Gibraltar Chronicle" published the following limerick.

Street Manners

"Here lie the bones of Michael O'Grady
"Who stepped off the path to make room for a lady
"In Gibraltar his action was thought so odd
"That a motocar sent him straight to his God".

These words mean and were intended to mean that Gibraltarians lack street manners, that unknown is the occasion when a gentleman steps off the path in Gibraltar to make room for a lady, and that such action in Gibraltar is in any case considered odd. I doubt if these words are capable of any other meaning, and since the Editor and Publishers decline to give any satisfaction, one must presume that they do not care what meaning can be put to these words nor whether the people feel hurt by these insinuations. It is not a bit difficult for me to guess who the author is, and I have not the slightest doubt but that the limerick was meant to hurt and to cause friction between the Gibraltarians and other British subjects.

The "Gibraltar Chronicle" is considered to be the official newspaper in Gibraltar. It is a periodical controlled exclusively by non-Gibraltarians. It publishes contributions from correspondents only after the proposed article for publication has received full consideration of the "controllers" and in some cases approval by "officials". The limerick was published unsigned and it must therefore be taken for granted that was editorial and that it received at least the "controllers" approval.

I deem it unnecessary at the moment to give more details than are necessary or relevant. The people of Gibraltar have no control over the "Gibraltar Chronicle" but they supply the cash. The Colonial funds keep the printing establishment busy all the year round, in fact, all Government work is done by the Garrison Library. Without such help, it would not be possible to run the business and far less to compete with private enterprise. Other local newspapers must depend on those who care to help and on many occasions publish Government notices free of charge.

Because the "Gibraltar Chronicle" is also the Official Gazette and is therefore in a privileged position, the people are under the obligation of purchasing the newspaper. Because such obligation exists, merchants, traders and others take advantage of such fact to put in their advertisements. The paper has therefore a forced wide circulation and the extent of the insult bears direct relation with the extent of such circulation.

The Government as the sponsors of the Gibraltar Chronicle Printing Office should realise that their duty is not solely administrative but must embrace «Empire making». That the said limerick will only lead to ill-feeling, and that that spirit of brotherhood between Great Britain and its Colonies which every member of the Cabinet is so eager to bring about will be seriously hampered by these irresponsibles who think nothing of biting the hand that feeds them.

It is the bounden duty of the Government to enquire into the circumstances in which such limerick was published, and further ascertain whether any Government official is involved. The people must not afterwards be accused of being unpatriotic or of being responsible for the existence of any ill-feeling. Provocation is the policy adopted by nonentities who are dumped into the colonies and constitute themselves «Empire breakers».

The Editor and Publishers of the "Gibraltar Chronicle" should read the Daily Mail of the 23rd. February last. Major A. C. Willison, Royal Tank Regiment, alleged in Salisbury Police Court that the town was inhospitable to troops. He complained about the reception he and his unit had been given and said they had been unable to get even a cup of tea after two days on the road. At once there were protests. Lieut-General Sir Bertie Fisher, General Officer Commanding-in-Chief, Southern Command sent Colonel the Right Hon. Earl Fortescue to the Mayor, to express regret at the unfortunate incident and to stress that the Southern Command Headquarters deeply appreciated the hospitality that Salisbury had always given to troops. Lt.-Col. E. F. Ledward officer commanding the battalion to which Major Willison was attached also called to express his battalion's regret. Is it possible, I ask, that that British spirit of fair play is left behind by some, when they move to a Colony?

L.

I never read the answer, for we had left Gibraltar by car to the U.K. We were on our way up, Hitler was about to make his way down.

SERENITY AND CONFIDENCE

By Beccles

After a week of real anxiety in which the constant thoughts of the people have been with the Allied Forces in Northern France, relief has at last come to us with the knowlegde that practically the whole of the Army has been saved. The success is reported to have been due to the co-operation of all the forces and the serenity and confidence displayed.

The Local Government acting on instructions received from the War Cabinet decided to evacuate women and children. No sooner was the decision published than arrangements were made for carrying it into effect. Success was dependent on the cooperation of everyone. The A. R. P. organization was made responsible for arrangements for evacuation. The Government chartered a large steamer to take over the evacuees to Morocco. Contact was made with the French authorities there. Simple as it looks, the work put in by all concerned is worthy of praise, and it seems to me that publicity should be given to what has turned out to be a real success.

Though the decision to evacuate caused dismay, for people are naturally reluctant to leave their homes, no one doubted that the Government was actuated by a sincere desire to protect the civil population from the horrors of war at a time when such evacuation could be carried out with ease and comfort and without endangering lives. In this spirit and with serenity and confidence every head of a family set out to make such arrangements as were necessary.

The Government sent representatives to Casablanca to make the necessary arrangements and the Chairman of the City Council and the Controller of the A. R. P. organization worked out the details of the scheme at this end.

I have often seen the embarkation of evacuees. With serenity and confidence the different groups were embarked. The efficiency with which it was done and the assistance given by members of the St. John Ambulance and the Police were worthy of admiration. All taxis and many private cars were used for the conveyance of evacuees and luggage to the wharf. These services as well as those rendered by many porters were free of charge. There are hardly words to express the gratitude of all for such devotion to humanity and kindness. The morale of all those who have gone, severing all connections not only with their dear ones but with the soil of their birth for God alone knows how long, has been truly wonderful and goes once again to show how truly British they all feel and the confidence they have in British methods and ways.

I went on board and saw the women and children sitting in the dining rooms. They all remained in the places assigned to them, not one word of protest but a tear, a sigh and many repressed emotions. Sweets and chocolates in large quantities contributed by the Mediterranean Racing Club were distributed among the children. His Excellency the Governor and Lady Liddell spoke to many of them and comforted the in their plight. Many other officials were also there. The great majority of this human cargo have never been on board a ship. They certainly knew not what sea-sickness was. Travelling with them were a doctor, Special Constables, members of the St. John Ambulance, voluntary nurses and group leaders.

I have not been privileged to travel on the steamer but I have been informed by many, that the officers on board were untiring in their efforts to make the evacuees as confortable as possible. Many words of praise have been uttered in respect of an officer who wears a monocle. He brings easy chairs to the weak and feeble, gives his own cabin to children and works with untiring efforts, for their general welfare. The heart of a good man is the sanctuary of God in this world. This officer has earned our deepest gratitude. What a consolation for those who still have to go to know in whose charge they will be during the trip.

In Morocco, Mr. Charles Gaggero, Mr. Joseph L. Imossi and staff work with unfailing interest in accommodating the evacuees. The French authorities are giving every facility to them. On arrival, the French Red Cross provide them with tea and biscuits. Tables are prepared at the wharf, and on disembarkation they are taken to their seats. The examination of the luggage is practically dispensed with. The sister of our French Consul has also earned everybody's gratitude for her unceasing efforts in providing comfort and asistance.

One can hardly expect accommodation to be an easy matter and consequently some have had to suffer inconvience for a little time. In the first place, the empty houses and flats are in different parts of the town. A group of persons must be given a flat with the necessary rooms to meet health requirements. They must be conveyed there. Sometimes the flat is too large for the persons who wish to live together, and other parties must be found to occupy it and vice-versa. When one considers the number of persons that must be accommodated, one realises how true are the reports that the staff is overworked and rendering services that money alone cannot pay. Moreover, Casablanca is not the only place where the evacuees are being sent. Many go to Rabat, Mazagan and Saffi, &c. Those who are left behind can be assured that their families will be well looked after during their enforced separation.

To make doubly sure that every effort is being made to give every comfort and assistance to our families, many prominent citizens have gone to Morocco on a tour of inspection, among them, the Chairman of the City Council, the Controller of A.R.P. the Medical Officer of Health and lately the Colonial Secretary. All express satisfaction on the admirable services that are being rendered by those who have been entrusted with the handling of evacuees.

But it must not be imagined that accommodation means furnished houses. Those who cannot afford to provide themselves with furniture can only be assisted to a very limited extent and only in special circumstances. The allowances are given are only sufficient for their ordinary needs. Many children will require extra feeding, substantial clothing, shoes &c. Mothers will require nourishment and some kind of home comforts. Many of those responsible for their maintenance will hardly be able to provide for them. They require our assistance and we are of course anxious that our hosts should not form a poor opinion of our efforts to keep our own folks clean and healthy. For these reasons and because our charitable institutions have always provided for their needs in Gibraltar, a relief fund is very necessary.

The Governor who has proved by his acts how much at heart he has the welfare of the people (he has already more than earned their gratitude) has formed a Committee for two purposes, first, to provide relief to those abroad and secondly to afford assistance to those left behind. The generosity of the people of Gibraltar has been proved time and again, and one cannot doubt that the call will be responded to the utmost of their power. I am glad to say that His Excellency has personally contributed £100 and thus by his generosity sets the example to us all. The funds of the Children's Poor Fund recently started to provide shoes and clothing to poor children will be transferred to the Relief Fund. Other contributions include £200 from Messrs. M. H. Bland & Co., Ltd. and £100 from the Mediterranean Racing Club.

Lady Liddell has kindly undertaken to form a Committee to assist those who are left behind by the organization of facilities to provide meals at cheap rates. Her interest in the welfare of the people has never been in doubt, and she can be assured of any assistance she may require.

The Gibraltar War Relief Fund is now the only assistance that can be given to our people in Morocco. Substantial sums are required and those who cannot afford to give a lump sum may give monthly contributions. In this respect, the Committee has been assured of a monthly subscription of £150 from the widow of that great benefactor and friend of the poor the late Mr. John Mackintosh.

Let us pray to God that this battle for life and civilization may soon come to a victorious termination, and that we may be spared to see the re-union of our families. That our serenity and confidence may never fail us.

In the evacuation speed was essential.

El Anunciador. *7 de Junio de 1940.*

L.

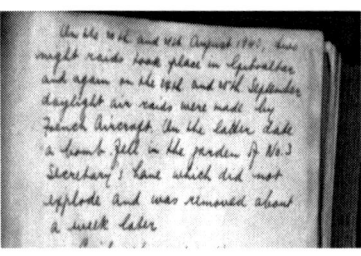

Our Lady of Europa Shrine at spot where bomb fell *(1940).*

Special Pass for District Commisioner *(1940).*

Emergency Powers Regulations *(1940).*

Chapter 5

STONYHURST COLLEGE. LONGRIDGE.

With our summer holidays over, we moved to our new wartime home in Longridge. It was called 'Broadfield', and lay at the periphery of this small Lancashire town (K 19). It was surrounded by fields, and the house was built from quarry stone. It had a low rental. It was offered for sale for nine hundred pounds, but the war situation was not good, and the money best kept, as fluid as possible. Broadfield was about 15 miles from Stonyhurst.

A few days at our new home and back to Hodder for the Christmas term. I had gone up one class and was now in its highest class: Figures. Whilst I was still the oldest boy in Figures, it was no longer in years but months.

Christmas 1940. Broadfield.

Our first Christmas at Broadfield was particularly dour and cold with several feet of snow blocking our backdoor entrance (K 13). At night we stayed in with our 'black-out blinds' firmly closed. Whenever light emitted from the house, an A.R.P. warden would call to warn us. We had to fix the problem immediately or face prosecution. We were rationed in meat, butter, cheese, bacon, eggs, sweets, chocolate, sugar, clothing and shoes (K 11). A host of other goodies were in short supply, including the turkey. Christmas 1940 was hardly a good one, but we were far better off than most Europeans on the continent.

The only warm room was the kitchen, with its old large coal-fired cooker. Gas was freely available. So we used hot baths to heat us up on very cold days. Coal, though not freely available, was never in short supply for it was used for cooking purposes only. All family members had to pitch in. I dried the plates and cutlery, made my bed and scrubbed the kitchen floors. I undertook errands to the town half a mile away. My father, aware of our love for cycling, had arranged for our cycles to be sent to Broadfield onboard the M.V. Neuralia from Gibraltar. The pleasure that cycling gave us, throughout the car free years in Longridge, was unimaginable. Without it, we would have been bored to death. We were constantly reminded that a Messerschmitt loitering in the sky could turn its guns on us, as it had done in France. We were to be always on the lookout for such planes when cycling in the country. With hindsight, this was virtually impossible, a bomber yes, but a fighter no.

During our first Christmas holiday, from 18 December 1940 to about 10 January 1941, from sunset to sunrise, we spent most of our sleeping time between our underground (and unused) wine cellar and the kitchen. The north blitz blazed across our skies. The Luftwaffe's prime targets were Liverpool, Manchester and the industrial North-West.

The roar of the bombers varied throughout these nights. The drone of the engines was easily identifiable when close above, but fortunately this was not often. When the 'all clear' sounded, usually just before dawn, we could see the candescent glow of a great fire on our southern horizon. Tired from our all-night vigil (and the occasional close loud bang) and with our water bottles well filled and hot, we then retired to bed. We were always relieved, that a German pilot had not released his unwanted bombs on us on his way home. It was not pleasant to see the horizon's red glow and to know of the many thousands now suffering, as we went to bed for a comfortable sleep. I offered a silent prayer for them.

I had always been a chocolate and sweets addict but my good family now no longer enjoyed them or at least, so they said. So the two ounces of sweets allowed per person per week became for me four as result of their generosity. This was my first Christmas holiday without my father but at least we were lucky, in so far as, we were all alive and well.

On my return to Hodder, I found I had made the Stonyhurst grade. I had spent two terms in the Preparatory class; one in Lower Elements; one in Upper Elements and two in Figures, when the average for all boys was three terms in each class. Within minutes of my arrival back at Hodder, I was taxied to Stonyhurst, but unfortunately still in my short trousers. Long trousers were worn at Stonyhurst. The matron, despite clothes rationing, quickly dealt with the problem and within 24 hours, I was in the 'The Long One'. My academia was now on track with my age. I was placed in Stonyhurst's lowest class, where the average age of 12 years and eight months was the same as mine.

Stonyhurst (M)

Stonyhurst, like Hodder was well organised, disciplined and highly efficient. Our lives were once again governed by bells. Every boy knew where to go when the first bell rang and by the time the second sounded five minutes later, one was in his place. The Jesuit or master would enter the classroom at the second bell. And if mass was to be said the priest would enter the church on time. Latecomers were punished and as a result, there were none. Punctuality was essential and insisted upon. The result was for all to see: a punctual and disciplined school.

There were two lines: Higher and Lower line. Higher was for the over sixteens. There were three playrooms, with number four being reserved for its youngest. There were four House lines which took their names from the school's history.

As F.D. of the Preston Guardian wrote "Stonyhurst was originally founded abroad to provide an education for Catholics whose schooling at home was rendered impossible by the penal laws. It was first established at St Omer in 1592 by Father Robert Persons. It carried on its work there through many vicissitudes, till it was forced by the French Government to seek an asylum in Bruges in 1762. Further troubles drove the establishment to Liege in 1773 and there it remained till the fury of the French Revolution expelled it from its home on the continent.

"Now among the schoolboys at the College in Bruges had been Thomas Weld of Lulworth, who in addition to extensive property in the South of England, was possessor of the Lancashire estate and mansion of Stonyhurst, on the slopes of Longridge Fell, overlooking lovely stretches of the Hodder and the Ribble, with Pendle Hill across the valley. He had not forgotten his old school, and in the hour of its distress, offered his northern house to be its new home.

"Hugh Shireburn, who died in 1527, made considerable additions, but the best known and most characteristic portion of the house was built by Sir Richard Shireburn, who succeeding to the property in 1537, held reign for 57 years. Towards the end of his life, he set about rebuilding the mansion of Stonyhurst on a scale of great magnificence, commencing the work by a curious coincidence, in 1592, the year that saw the first beginning at St Omer of the College, one day to enjoy the fruits of his labours". The names of the lines took their name from Stonyhurst history: Shireburn, Weld and St Omer, but there was another one in Campion. He was one of the English Jesuit martyrs: Blessed Edmund Campion. The Isolas' family line was Shireburn.

Dormitories were large, with many individual cubicles and occupied according to age. Higher Line had individual rooms. The wash-room was huge and reserved for Lower Line. Every boy had his own wash-basin and locker. Following mass at 8.00 a.m., breakfast was served. Afterwards to the study room for morning studies. During this time your class was called to the toilets, which were large. They contained 60-plus individualised toilets under one roof. The senior classes were called first. By the time the most junior class made its way to the 'Bogs', as it was known, there was a distinct bad odour! This diminished as you aged and progressed upwards. Next to the 'Bogs' was the Ambulacrum; a roofed football ground with compressed mud for a floor. Indoor games and other events took place there. The heated swimming pool was massive by most standards. On one side lay the showers, which were mainly used after rugger or any other outdoor sports and prior to a swim. Individualised baths were at the other end, for the weekly scrub down. The question of how heated the pool was, depended on whether you came from Aberdeen or Gibraltar, but once submerged, was pleasant for all. It certainly was warmer than the Hodder River.

STONYHURST COLLEGE.   M.

An aeriel view of Stonyhurst. In the background is St. Marys, which during World War II was the home of the Venerable English College in Rome.

A view from my room. *(1944).*

The Quadrangle.

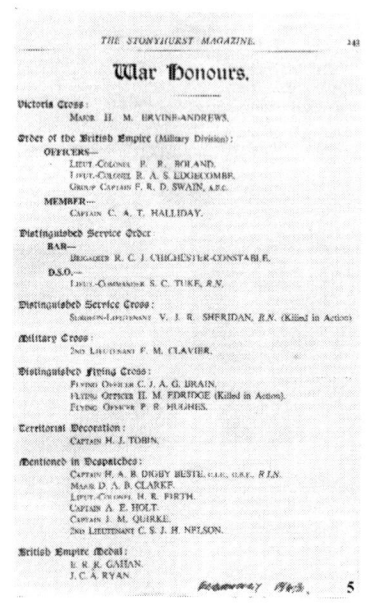

From the pond.

War honours.

Behind the infirmary.

Stonyhurst and the War: Roll of Honour

M.

KILLED IN ACTION.	WOUNDED.
Surgeon-Lieut. V. J. R. SHERIDAN, D.S.C., R.N.	Major F. R. HULTON.
Sub-Lieut. E. L. PHILLIPS, R.N.V.R.	Capt. LORD ARUNDELL OF WARDOUR (Prisoner of War).
Major C. H. J. CHICHESTER-CONSTABLE, M.C.	Capt. G. W. CARRINGTON.
	Capt. J. B. S. PAYNE.
Capt. J. J. B. JACKMAN. V.C.	Capt. P. J. FAWDRY.
Lieut. A. G. HICKSON.	Lieut. H. H. W. DUFFY.
2nd Lieut. D. R. WARD.	2nd Lieut. H. A. JONES (Prisoner of War).
Cpl. F. G. COLLINGWOOD.	Flight Lieut. H. DE G. DOMVILLE.
Sqdn. Ldr. D. Y. FEENY.	
Flight Lieut. H. M. FERRISS, D.F.C.	**PRISONERS OF WAR.**
Pilot Off. H. P.M. EDRIDGE.	Major W. H. HAROLD.
Pilot Off. R. S. C. N. St. JOHN-SPENCER.	Major W. P. JONES.

Stonyhurst and the War: Roll of Honour. *(February 1942).*

THE SHIREBURN ARMS HOTEL

Higher Line steeplechase. Writer arrowed.

The Refectory.

Corpus Christi. High mass at St. Peter's Church. *(1943).*

As a result of the shortage of servants, the boys now make their own beds between Mass and breakfast. As a further result three boys began in November to serve six of the tables in the Refectory at all meals.

The War effort.

M.

Grammar Play. "All women are men" (1944).

The Academy Room.

Lower Grammar. (1942).

During the early part of November the boys in their classes helped with the potato picking, and altogether £36 12s. was paid out in wages while about 110 tons of potatoes were lifted in ten days.

The War effort.

Visits to the matron were obligatory for Stonyhurst's youngest members. Radio Malt (Vitamin A & D), which was delicious or Cod Liver Oil, which was not, was given to the youngest members of the school or those who were constantly ill. Those with a temperature were admitted to the infirmary. In keeping with Victorian habits that 'clean bowels make healthy men', a purgative was given to all who were constipated for 24 hours. Purgation Friday consisted of Milk of Magnesia, Syrup of Figs or Liquid Paraffin. Many people at the time believed in Castor Oil, as the panacea to a healthy life.

The study place was very large by any standards, encompassing more than 300 individualised desks, each bearing one's name and year of entry on a brass plate. Previous old boys 'brass plates covered the desks' front view. I could identify my father's and other previous old boy's desks, by searching. Major Ervine Andrews V.C. left a white crispy £5 note in the desk he had sat in, years earlier, to the delight of the new incumbent.

There were four class periods in the morning, lasting three quarters of an hour each, separated by a half hour break, and three in the afternoon. In the evening we had homework.

Lunch was three course, and always acceptable, but it never compared with home. There was plenty of milk for consumption. Once a week, my allowable butter ration was served at breakfast and consumed on one slice of bread. For the rest of the week I had to do without. Those who preferred to use it sparingly were often rewarded by their butter turning rancid in our centrally heated school. It had to be consumed within 24 hours for optimum taste.

My evenings were directed to study and evening prayers in the chapel. Lights out by 9.00 p.m. The mattress was hard, yet I always had a very good sleep. Every Thursday afternoon, without fail, was reserved for O.T.C. (Officer Training Corps) training. We were at war and our cadet training was targeted towards that goal. Discipline, smartness, and good drill were essential. When on parade, there was nothing more frightening than to hear one's name bellowed out by a former regimental sergeant major of the Irish Guards. On one occasion, in front of the whole school, which was on parade in the quadrangle (M3), I heard his voice bellow "E . . . SO . . . LA two paces forward: march" and you did. This was followed by a tirade of undecipherable words. It was frightening.

Friday was fish-day, and was the only day in which the food was unacceptable, but you had to eat it. Yet the fish at any Lancashire 'Fish & Chip' shop was delicious. Why could my College not do likewise? There was a war on.

The notice board outside the chapel was reserved for the names of those who had been killed in action or had died of war wounds (M 7). Some were known to me, as they were in Higher Line when I entered College. We had two Victoria Crosses awarded to Stonyhurst boys: Major Irvine Andrews at Dunkirk (M 5) and Captain Jackman (M 7) in Libya. The former survived and a holiday to celebrate his valour was enjoyed by all.

Every year, I went up one class. By 1944 Science was about to enter the school's curriculum in earnest. Latin and Greek were two of the main subjects taught. In 1944 my class was given the choice of whether or not we wished to take Latin as a subject for the Oxford and Cambridge School certificate. By a substantial majority, the class voted democratically against the subject's inclusion. Without it, I could not enter a medical school. I left

Stonyhurst in 1945, following my matriculation, in order to prepare for my Latin examination, which I took and passed five months later.

Wartime schooling was enjoyable, despite the many deprivations that existed during my time. It gave one a solid background, and when I compared myself with those less fortunate, the education at Stonyhurst was outstanding. Boredom did not exist, for you were kept busy one way or another. Freedom to roam was very much restricted, though in my last year, I found ways of bypassing the system and fortunately was never caught!

I boxed for Stonyhurst and never won a fight, principally because of my weight, resulting in an older boy, as my opponent. It usually was the fight of the night, shared with Leo McParland. It certainly raised the audience's bellows. In Rugby, my sport career was less illustrious. I only played for the 3rd fifteen. I won the chess championship in Lower line (2nd Playroom), and I might have won it in Higher line, had there been one to contest.

Some of the wartime clubs that emerged in 1943 lacked the essentials for them to succeed. The Photography Club without cameras could never be a success. Bar the Kodak Box camera, which was difficult to buy, there were no others on the market. The Dancing Club, which most of us hoped would result in one nearby convent school partaking, never materialised, despite our mild protestations. Instead a Jesuit showed us the steps required for each particular dance, with an antique gramophone, old needles and equally old records. It might have been a success had the nearby convent joined in. It did not! In the Tennis Club, we were restricted to old rackets and tennis balls that had already served out their lives years earlier. Many balls simply died on the court and new ones were unobtainable. 'There is a war on!' So most of the clubs gradually fizzled out, for it was felt that the clubs were more of theoretical than practical value

Punishment for those who erred consisted of the ferula or pink paper. Their use was generally restricted to fooling, disobedience, bad behaviour or manners. It was rarely meted out for poor academia. The times for the ferula were at 1.00 p.m. and 8.45 p.m. and always in room number 10. The pain was more in the waiting than in the hand application. The antidote: a basin full of hot water. Within 10 minutes of dipping your hands, the pain receded and your hands became mobile. Within the hour you felt a lot better though writing was difficult. By the end of the day you were ready to re-offend. Few did!

It was in the pink paper, as a form of punishment, where problems usually arose, for it was a time-consuming punishment, which dug well into your free time. As the paper was pink, it was easily identifiable by the supervising Jesuit. It could not be used in the study or class room. The penalty when caught was double the lines plus an aperitif of 9 ferulas. It was therefore done outside study hours, which was wasteful if you had better things to do, which most of us had. The lines had to be well written, and the paper had to be clean when presented, with no ink-smudges.

In one of my school reports, not good on this occasion, the words 'Cecil very trying' appeared under 'Comments'. My mother interpreted this statement in a very different way and wired my father with the words 'Cecil trying very hard'. It resulted in my father giving me a 'white £5 note' as an encouragement to my further 'trying'!

Longridge

By 1943 peace reigned in our Longridge area. With empty roads, other than for buses, doctors and a few others, cycling as a means of transport could not have been bettered. We were allowed to travel a four mile radius for our cycling needs. There were no sign posts, maps and many of the street names had been removed in order to thwart any parachuted German spy. Uncle Tuto, despite his severe asthma, had decided to help in the war effort. He had applied for a foundry job, a quarter mile away from home. Within a few weeks of employment, he was struck by such a severe attack that he was close to death. He was obviously unfit for any war-time service so took a sedentary job with the C.W.S.

My Aunt Kittita, in 1938, had attended the May Day Great Labour demonstration in Hyde Park, to hear speakers of the calibre of Professor Laski, Emmanuel Shinwell, Herbert Morrison, Edith Summerskill and a host of others. Eighty bands led the procession to the six areas with eight platforms. As she had early Otosclerosis, she stood near one of the many loudspeakers. A 'blue stocking' and a supporter of Christian values, she was also a paid up member of the British Labour Party. Two years later, two Spanish Civil War refugees, now members of the British Communist Party and living in Liverpool, sought our help. The Communist Party was petitioning the British government to seek peace with Germany. At the time the Soviet Union and Germany had a non-aggression pact. Kittita and her sisters were asked to sign the petition and to attend the Liverpool Peace Demonstration. They declined. A follow up visit by M.I.5. resulted. They were interested in the peace makers and what they said. No further visits occurred by either for they were satisfied by their answers. Poor Kittita was scolded, by her two sisters, for being the cause of the M.I.5.'s unwanted visit (K 14).

With our first Christmas in Britain blemished by the Luftwaffe, the third was marred by my mother's admission to hospital for an undiagnosed ailment. We were able to visit her on a daily basis, as a result of the Ribble Bus: excellent service. She remained in hospital during the whole of our Christmas holidays.

My father, who we had not seen for three years, appeared unexpectedly during our summer vacation. He had come to the U.K. on urgent Government business. Crossing the Strait on Bland's ferry, he had flown from Tangier to Lisbon. Seated on the London-bound plane, ready for take off, he was asked to vacate his seat for a V.I.P. and take another flight. He learnt on his return to Secretary's Lane that the plane he was originally booked for was missing and all the passengers were presumed dead. The plane was never found. No reasons were given as to its loss. He was lucky.

His one and only wartime visit was short-lived, but during that time Peter and I accompanied him to London. There were a few air-raid warnings, but the Londoners were now well acclimatised after the Blitz. Air-raid warnings on the cinema screen were ignored by cinema goers. We saw and heard the VI (Doodlebug) fly in the sky. The most frightening and deafening sound came from the unexpected V2 exploding. We heard it once and we presumed it was a V2, for there was no air-raid warning, but a very, very large shuddering explosion. We saw the devastation caused there from the top of a double-decker bus. Piccadilly Circus was like an American military camp. The Americans outshone the British army, not only in the quality of their uniform, but in their numbers. The London I knew as a boy had changed forever.

Boating in the Serpentine was restricted to half an hour; just in case. Large numbers of Barrage Balloons adorned the London sky. Night walks were difficult to enjoy due to the blackout.

My father's stay was short but enjoyable. He now no longer smoked, for he had had a massive heart attack at age 43. The advice given was to stop his daily 80 cigarette consumption completely: he did from day one. And as he left for Gibraltar, he handed us a large box of Cadbury's chocolates. At Stonyhurst life continued in the usual way, but we were kept so busy that as the years rolled on, the terms seemed to get shorter. The 'Daily Express' became my second Bible, for it was the paper that headlined the 'good news' best: the Battle of Britain, El Alamein and the sinking of the Bismarck. With the good news came the bad: the sinking of the Hood, Ark Royal, Repulse, Rawalpindi and others sunk by Japanese kamikaze. Most, if not all, of the British warships that were to meet this gloomy fate had called at Gibraltar prior to 1940, and were well known to us children.

As the war progressed, good news came more regularly: D-Day landing, Stalingrad, and others. In the North, we could now roam freely. We had good neighbours in the Wallbanks and Carters, and with Coleridge to take us around. Johnnie Stagnetto, now at Stonyhurst, joined the Broadfield family for two years whilst on holidays. The war, for us, was over by 1943, except for rationing.

When war finally ended, we were expecting it. A march down Ave Maria Avenue (M 2) by the whole school to celebrate 'Victory' was impressive and a few days holiday spent with Alderman Wright at his home was one of many celebration parties. Eight weeks later, examinations finished, I saw the College for the last time. Did I enjoy it? Yes. Did it make me a better man? Yes. Would I have recommended this school to my children? Yes. My own sons, Brian, Richard, Michael and Mark followed in my footsteps years later.

Prior to saying my goodbye, I looked at the two windows of my room, on the second floor above the front gate. What a beautiful view I had from that room. But unfortunately it took me years before I realised it. Such views, like youth, are often wasted on the young.

Returning Home

Back in Longridge, we began to pack and get ready to go home. Problems created by the war; transport and sea mines prevented us from enjoying our 1945 summer holiday in Gibraltar. The Lancashire people were undoubtedly the friendliest people one could meet on the mainland. Our school holidays could not have been more enjoyable.

There was one last thing we had to know before leaving Lancashire for good. The General Election was on and though none of us had a vote, nonetheless, we were interested in the result, for Winston Churchill's son Randolph, was the Conservative candidate for Preston. He was defeated by the Labour candidate. 'Time to leave England. The place is going red' said my mother. We witnessed the result outside Preston's Town Hall. Many of those who spoke at the Great Labour Rally of 1938 now formed part of Clement Attlee's post-war government.

My mother had a great fear of communism, mainly as a result of the many atrocities, committed by all sides in the Spanish Civil War. With Randolph's demise, her new horizon was Christmas in Gibraltar. By September, my extended family had returned home.

My mother stayed on in London, for the new surgical procedure for her deafness (Otosclerosis) now in vogue. To this end, the surgeon, Mr Passe performed a 'Fenestration Operation'. It was not a success. In October 1945 my mother and sister returned to Gibraltar, and I undertook a five month Latin course at the 'Chestnuts' in Henley-on-Thames.

Chapter 6

PEACE

No Latin—no university. Latin was the subject sought by all universities, and without it, there was no hope of being admitted to medical school. My good school friend, Alex Meldrum, had applied to Trinity College, Dublin and had been accepted. He lived in Merrion Square, a short distance from the College. I had heard of the world-ramous Rotunda Hospital and of the excellent School of Physics at Trinity.

In 1944, I applied to Guy's Hospital medical school London and was interviewed but was not accepted. I was three hours late for my appointment. I arrived just as the Admissions Board were at the door, ready to leave. "If you cannot arrive on time for an interview" they said "you will arrive late for an appendix operation with devastating effects on the patient". I had a fairly good excuse for being late. I had arrived from the north the previous day, and though I had a fair idea, where the hospital was, I had been slowed down by two air-raid warnings, which necessitated I take cover for 90 minutes.

My attempts to obtain direction: first to the hospital and then to the interview room failed, due to a non-co-operative war-footing public. Posters all over London warned the public not to be loose with their tongue. 'CARELSS TALK COSTS LIVES' and 'THE ENEMY HAVE EARS' and so on. There were no London maps in wartime Britain, which might have helped both 'the enemy' and me to locate the hospital. As a schoolboy, I was expected to use the bus service.

I was fortunate enough not to have been accepted at Guys, for had I been, I might not have applied to Trinity and as a result would never have met my future wife May. My Trinity application was accepted and a place reserved at the medical school for the 1947 Michaelmas term with certain provisos. I had to pass the Oxford and Cambridge matriculation and with a credit or above in Latin. I had to wait two years.

Places for all medical schools were difficult to come by, due to the number of servicemen returning from the war's operational zones. Priority for places went to them, provided they had their school certificates in order. Most had. By the time I left Stonyhurst, I had my matriculation. All I now needed was Latin.

The post-war bulge for university entrance had a three to four year lag, with priority given to returning and demobbed servicemen. Competition for university places was brisk. I had my eyes fully focussed on Ireland and nothing would deter me from that course.

Henley-on-Thames

I left Stonyhurst in the summer of '45 a few months before the United States detonated two atomic bombs on Japan. I was then seventeen years old. My last summer at Broadfield was one to be remembered, for Europe though devastated, was now at peace. The weather in Lancashire that summer was perfect. Willie, now at Oxford, had identified a 'private' school, in Henley-on-Thames, which he believed would suit my 'Latin' curriculum ends. My Latin tutor would be an Oxford don, who was well past middle age. Within six months, he guaranteed a credit in Latin with a one hour lesson per day. Had I not been so determined to pass my Latin examination, I would have failed, for the teaching was nowhere near the quality experienced at Stonyhurst.

Two Gibraltarians joined me, whose fathers were my father's clients: Mario Mifsud and Joseph Perea. Their education had been badly affected by the problems that go with a war and an attempt was now being made to put matters right. They had the benefit of my experience to ensure them a soft landing in a "regulated" house and in an educational system unknown to them.

All the war-time restrictions were still in place. Blackouts were a thing of the past and I no longer feared a German plane swooping down behind me after 1943. Henley became central to my recreation, for I enjoyed boating on the river. My one attempt on a single scull ended in the cold river and a good swim to its bank. The roads like in the north-west, were virtually car free due to petrol rationing and no cars. All new cars were being exported to world markets. Long cycle rides, mainly solo, gave me a good feel for the countryside and its unspoilt beauty. There was little evidence in this area of the Luftwaffe's excesses.

The tutor's wife was our cook and considering there was still rationing, did particularly well. On one occasion, she introduced as part of her menu a heart. At first we all felt squeamish, but on her insistence, we tasted it. Its flavour was good and as a result it formed par of our bi-monthly menu. After leaving Henley I never tasted such a 'delicacy' again. In a Henley restaurant, David Fettes, a Baghdadian, complained to management that the rabbit we had eaten was a cat. It probably was. He wanted to 'analyse' its bones and asked for a suitable bottle to carry them in. By the time we left, he had ensured one less friendly restaurant, in an area where they were few and far between.

Exeats: Oxford and Victory Parade

Permission to stay out the night was rarely refused. We were at the 'age of reasoning.' On the few occasions that I sought an exeat, I always returned with a memory never to be forgotten. Willie had arranged a cocktail party, to which I had been invited, prior to Pembroke College's Summer Ball, Oxford (N.3.).

All the undergraduates in our party were trying to impress the opposite sex, and I was no exception. In order to show one girl my macho and rowing skills, I invited her to a row on the River Isis the next day. She accepted. Unfortunately the boat on which I could show her my macho skills was unobtainable. A punt was the only boat available. I took it, even though I had never punted before. So what: I was 'das beste.' My lady friend sat comfortably and faced her all conquering 'macho' punter. She was happy. It was so easy to punt, until an unknown punter had the cheek to overtake me. This was unacceptable. Speed was now essential, if I was to overtake this braggart. Unfortunately, my pole stuck deep into the river bed and left me dangling, whilst my lady friend continued her onward journey: 'solo' in the punt. Slowly but surely to the amusement of many of the bank's onlookers, gravity took its part, and I, 'The

Venetian', ended horizontally in the cold River Isis, fully clothed. While my companion comforted me with a grin, she would not allow me to accompany her back to St Hilda's College. Not only did I look like a wet rag, but felt like one. My one day love affair 'to be' had ended: permanently. Crestfallen, I returned to Henley.

The Victory Parade

My other escapade was to attend London's Victory Parade (N 6), which took place on the 8 June 1946. I was up very early and took the train from Henley to London's Paddington Station, arriving at 9 a.m. Traffic was chaotic due to the hundreds of thousands that had invaded the capital to watch the victory spectacle, for that is what it was to be. The quickest way to 'The Mall' was on foot. I was well attired for the occasion with a good mackintosh: a must in the English Summer.

By the time I reached 'The Mall', the crowds must have been twelve deep along the parade route. There was little chance of pushing my way through, especially since many had camped there since the day before. There were plenty of trees to climb and from my O.T.C. training, I was well versed on how best to achieve it. Unfortunately there were plenty of policemen about and in 1946 respect for them was paramount. I would have to wait for the parade to start and then act when there was little chance of being spotted. My opportunity came just as the most fantastic parade that I or anybody else would ever see, began. As an ape would, I hopped up and for the next one and a half hours sat on The Mall's most restful tree. Perched high up and well hidden from the ground, I watched the Victory Parade, comfortably seated and with a perfect view. In this historic victory march past, regiment after regiment; band after band; nation after nation; the Empire and Commonwealth and many others, filed. It was truly magnificent, but shortly before the end, a constable with radar eyes ended my balcony view, calling me down. After the parade, there was a great human surge towards Buckingham Palace, where the King and Queen, their Princesses and Winston Churchill appeared on the balcony: not once but several times.

All the restaurants appeared closed. They would have been packed. Fortunately the street vendors were out in force, selling their hot dogs by the ton. Sweets were still on ration and few outlets would have been around selling them. I saw none. After the parade, what intrigued me most, was a member of the A.T.S. (Auxiliary Territorial Service) standing upright and close to one of the lions at Trafalgar Square. Standing to this woman's right, was a long queue of men; some in uniform, others not. She was offering her red lips to kiss for a limited time, as part of her contribution to Victory Day. I accepted her kind offer for three seconds: no overtime.

By the time I realised that it was time to go home, at about 12.30 a.m. the next day, the bus and train services had ceased. Though it was 'Victory Day', the bus and train crews had to have their rest. Hundreds of thousands were left stranded around Central London. I was one of the 'lucky' ones.

London after midnight with nowhere to go or eat can be quite unnerving especially on a rainy night in Trafalgar Square. By 2 a.m. some of the Trafalgar flags were pulled down and used as pillows and blankets by the thousands of revellers who had been left stranded. By 5.30 am., the cold night air began to bite. Drizzly rain made matters worse. I was now looking for heat, and the

Trafalgar lion that had given me a few hours rest, with considerable discomfort, was now no longer of any use. Walking down Whitehall near Parliament Square, I saw a gent's toilet. It was beautifully warm and in keeping with the throngs on the streets above, packed. I bought three Sunday papers. I put a penny in the toilet's slot and with three Sunday newspapers for my cushion, I entered the sitting and warm area of an English lavatory, ready for a good night's sleep. But not for long, for the attendant climbed a small ladder to see what this man was up to. I was in dream world, warm and fast asleep. With a loud and aggressive voice, he shouted "you there, this is a place for s . . . . , not sitting. Get out or I'll call the police." I left, before he could set eyes again on me. I walked on through a devastated and badly bombed Victoria. At its unscathed end was what I believed to be a large synagogue. The door was open. It was empty and there were plenty of seats available. It was warm. I sat in an area where Jewish worshippers would not have been offended. To sit down and a snooze was all I needed. Three hours later, I was awoken by the chruchgoers leaving the church. I was in Westminster Cathedral.

From there to Paddington railway station by foot, was but a stone's-throw for me. I had intended to lunch at Henley, but missed my connection at Twyford due to my second sleep. I was awakened at Oxford by the station's loud speaker. "This is Orrxford . . . ." I jumped off and onto another train this time in the opposite direction. I finally arrived in Henley, just in time for supper.

Within six months of moving to Henley, I had the necessary credit in Latin. I could now relax and enjoy Henley's rowing and cycling amenities. I returned to Gibraltar for my summer holidays, fully relaxed from a three months no-work atmosphere, my last.

Travelling Home, Christmas 1945

The pre-war ease with which one could travel from Gibraltar to Britain was over by 1939. In Christmas 1945, a group of students including the writer, travelled by train and ferry from London to Irun via Paris, as this was the only way for us to reach Gibraltar. Paris like London was full of military uniforms and everything was in short supply. The leader of the pack suggested a night club for eating and as most of us were mugs, (under 19 and male) we agreed.

I followed the leader for I was two years younger than him and equally naïve. The night club was small and empty, for we had arrived too early. As the war had just ended, we were aware of food shortages, everywhere. We therefore ordered whatever was available on the menu, in our best schoolboy French. Tomatoes and lettuce without dressing was all that was available. This was to be our first post-war Parisienne meal. Following the first cabaret act, our 'experienced' leader suggested to the ladies that they should join us. They did! Since there were not enough chairs they sat on our laps. We were thrilled by our 'conquest'. As we could not entertain our 'Entente Cordiale' friends with 'still water', the first bottle of Champagne was ordered, to celebrate the mugs' victory. By the time we left the club, I had enough cash left to pay for one bottle of water and a loaf of bread. The next day we travelled by train to Irun. Fortunately I had paid all my expenses 'up front' and with Pedro Russo's chauffeured car awaiting us at Irun, 36 hours later, I could survive. I learnt my lesson! The Spain of 1940, had not improved much. Hunger was still rampant; poverty extreme and there was an over-abundance of police and military uniforms.

On our way down the Iberian Peninsula, we eventually arrived at the small and smelly fishing port of Estepona. From there we could see the Rock, in the distance. What cheered us most, two and a half hours later, was the Union Jack, proudly fluttering at the frontier gates. As we got closer, we saw Gibraltar's bobbies and the frontier's military guard. We had made it and now were about once again to regain paradise, after five long years in exile. Gibraltar like London and Paris was teeming with servicemen, except that here, the civilians appeared to be in the minority.

In keeping with my father's 'Welcome Home' traditions, Salvador of Hulhoven's hairdresser awaited us in the bathroom for our welcome haircut. On every occasion, until my marriage in 1956, Salvador was there, to ensure that our hair was of the acceptable social style. On this occasion our clothes were not up to post-war Gibraltar standards. There was no rationing here. We sported worn out shoes and collars; patched jackets and trousers; holed socks; all as a result of five years clothes' rationing in Britain. Fortunately the enterprising Garcia brothers of Main Street took their business seriously. They were well placed, for an over-zealous and victorious British Government was now in full-gear to regain her pre-war eminence in trade. It was now exporting many of her wares, often unobtainable and rationed in Britain, including clothing. Wealthy and pro-Franco Spaniards obtained the necessary entry and exit visas and bought well. He therefore had a good turn-over. For us it was manna from heaven, since we were informed of the merchandise's arrival, immediately. We had an excellent tailor in Algeciras. He performed miracles in order to please his new clientele. We soon were once again as well dressed as the American servicemen in London and resident Gibraltarians. We looked and felt good. The clothes coupon was over for us, but the coupon book could not be destroyed, for in that book, sweets, sugar, butter etc were still required on our return to the U.K.

My boyhood friends of 1939 now wore long trousers and were young men. And the girls were now young ladies. Christmas 1945, was one of celebration with parties galore and a return to civilisation. For many of us, it was to be our first Christmas celebration since 1939 and for us something more: re-union with my father, his parents and their families. The Christmas lunch was attended by 18 of us. The food was superb. Christmas gifts were not exchanged. This came later, on 6 January 1946. We returned to what was unavailable to us in England: the midnight Christmas Mass and the New Year Eve's Te Deum at the Cathedral of St Mary the Crowned.

My father believed, quite rightly, that major educational experiences must never be missed. With the brigadier's help, the second-in-command of the fortress, he arranged a tour for Peter and me inside the Rock by a major in his military driven jeep. We started at Fortress Headquarters (F.H.Q.). Our tour of war tunnels lasted several hours. All the military areas were still in functioning mode, as if the war was still on. In the huge R.E.M.E. chambers, which were floodlit, lorries and jeeps were being repaired. I saw what Hitler would like to have seen, had the post-war German documents held at F.H.Q. come to fruition. Bearing in mind, the capture of Singapore, I asked a question as we left the miles of underground tunnels and man-made caves. "With the benefit of hindsight and with the documents now held, do you think the Germans could have captured The Rock?" "Maybe" was the major's reply.

Six years is a long time without seeing your family and friends, and fortunately for us, only our Great-Aunt Clementine did not return from the forced exile. She was buried in Jamaica: one of the many places where Gibraltarians had been evacuated to in 1940.

During the war-years, I met no girls in Longridge, but in Gibraltar the girlies of 1939, had now become 1945 ladies and beautiful at that. There was no problem in meeting them, for I knew them all. The difficulty was in the dating. From 1945 to the year I met my future wife in 1952, the ratio of men to women here, was probably about 10 to 1. The British Empire was at its peak. Cocktail parties abounded not only on warships and private homes, but in the military messes as well. The war was over and peace was being celebrated on a daily basis and in my case during my vacation time as well. For the women living in Gibraltar, it was a golden era. Those women who I wished to date followed a pattern; their hand-bag opens; out comes the pen; engagement diary opened; "fully booked for the month". I saw it. Something had to be devised. Willie was prepared to lend me his car and as cars were in short supply, I now had a small advantage over the others. "Would you like to come dancing to the Reina Christina in Algeciras after your dinner date?" Few refused. I had beaten the system!

Comparisons are odious, but the Christmas of 1945, held no similarity whatever between my life in Gibraltar and that of the U.K. Everything was available here. There was no rationing. There was however no fresh milk, only tinned. We were at peace, at home, and in a warm and safe environment. What better than that? But we were restricted in time, for we were only on holidays, and sooner rather than later, would have to return to a peaceful Britain with its rationing and shortages.

London

London during the period 1946-7 was still suffering from the effects of war. Unlike the warm people of the north, they were cold. There was no way, I could expand my mind or girth through travelling abroad, as Europe was devastated. Transport was difficult and there were world-wide pockets of resistance within the Empire to British rule. As I had passed all the necessary examinations required for university admission, there was nothing left for me, but to brush up on my science subjects, which would eventually be required at university level. To this end an excellent school of tutors, by name 'Davis, Dick and Laing' filled my gap year. Most of the students that I met were marking time, prior to their university admission.

El Calpense

GIBRALTAR (17/7/45)

THE ELECTIONS

BY BECCLES

Very wisely it has been decided that the City Council should be completely disassociated from politics. The Council is in effect a cooperative trading concern in which we are all shareholders. What we require on the Council are men of experince and ability, individually pledged to endeavour to increase the prestige and activities of the Council to cooperate to the utmost in solving our Housing Problem, so that our people can return as quickly as possible; to raise our standard of wages; to reduce the price of Electricity, Gas and Water and restore the pre-war standard of cleanliness of our streets.

Gibraltar is small enough for us to know the Candidates individually and not to require party labels. We have all had plenty of examples of the dangers of allowing discontent and resentment to be exploited so that a blank cheque is given for nebulous policies of which no details are given. We have seen the disadvantages of having Candidates responsible to a Party Committee. For example, any candidate who stands as a representative of the A.A.C.R. would be automatically pledged to support any scheme approved by them. One of their schemes was to form a Housing Pool. Did everyone fully realise what this scheme meant? Let us examine it in detail.

If a man with his wife and two children lived in a flat consisting of four rooms and a kitchen, he would be required to give up one of the rooms in order to put in two adults either by subletting the room or billeting them. The obvious result would be communal living by Gibraltarians, the end of privacy and a home, and the adoption of ideas which are foreign not only to us but to the British Empire. "A man's home is his castle" must be the guiding factor in all questions affecting housing.

I wonder how many of us are contented with the state of affairs brought about by the adoption of the policy of housing people in other people's homes, removing furniture from them and storing them in Waterport, and generally interfering with a person's private property. Many have no doubt gained by the adoption of such a policy but I wonder how they would feel if this same policy was now adopted in their case.

There appears to be no doubt that the evacuees in Northern Ireland or at least the great majority of them had their flats or houses in Gibraltar before they left. Why can't they come back? Because their homes cannot be restored to them. The A.A.C.R. whilst doing their utmost to bring them back, have in fact supported such a disastrous policy and now suggest a housing pool as a remedy.

I fail to see how the candidates put forward by the A.A.C.R. can oppose the policy adopted by the Association. If they do it, it is a different matter, in which case the vote should be cast for the individual. But if the A.A.C.R. candidates support a policy of communal living, then I fail to see how a voter can cast his vote for them if he has any regard for his home.

Housing is the most important issue, and the City Council is interested in this issue. I will vote for the candidate who will disassociate himself from a policy which has had such disastrous consequences.

In effect, the only way to keep the City Council out of politics is not to vote for a Party but for an individual. It is impossible to have a Party representing the whole town; the idea is impractical and undemocratic. Remember that we have not had an election for a long time and that it is more essential than ever that we should have men of experience, character, ability and independence. This is the test on which will depend to what extent we will be entrusted with conducting our own affairs. Therefore, use your vote and see that the Candidates give you the necessary pledges, and choose the ablest and most experienced individuals available irrespective of labels.

A disastrous policy for the many but not for the few.

N.

PEACE 1945-47

N.

Family re-union. Christmas. *(1945)*.

Air crash in Madrid. Next morning.

Pembroke College, Oxford. *(1946)*

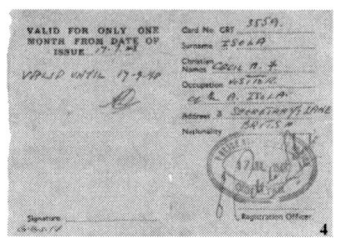

Identity card.
I was a visitor to my city.

Victory Parade.
London. *(1946)*

The Victors.

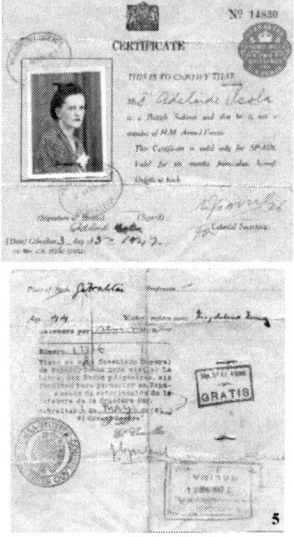

Daily pass for Spain. The request.

There were no visible changes between wartime and the peaceful London of 1946, except there were now, no air-raids or Doodle-bugs to worry about. American servicemen were still plentiful. Wherever they went, they drew attention; not only by their loud voices, but by the smart and well-tailored uniforms they wore. As for the British people they were still on clothes' rationing, and one could see the marked differences between them and other nationals. I was by now, thanks to the Garcia brothers as well-dressed, as the Americans. But when it came to competing with them on the few occasions that I went to the Hammersmith Palais, they won, hands down. They had in excess what no British or European had: the almighty dollar. And for the girls, they had silk or nylon stockings, cigarettes and candy, not available to most of us in the U.K. There were odd exceptions to the rule. One such was a Gibraltarian, who not only was beautiful, but intellectually supreme. We got on well in the dance-hall and as a result I walked her home. She knew a Gibraltarian who looked and spoke like me, and whose name was Willie Isola. Did I know him? I did not, even though he was my brother. For reasons best known to myself, I kept my identity and residency close to my chest. I never wanted any form of relationship that would lead me to marriage, before I completed my medical studies.

A decade plus, later, she called at my surgery for a consultation. Not only did I have a photographic memory for faces, but this patient had one as well. Roars of laughter were all that my secretaries could hear. I had been identified. The adolescent blush that had fortunately left me in my teens, now returned with a vengeance but this time I went purple. She still lives in the U.K.

The pre-war restaurants where my father took us as youths, when good food was wasted on us, had now gone downhill.

Whereas the food eaten at home, (in Gibraltar) in the pre and post-war years was superb, the food in post-war London was no better than that eaten during the war. I invariably ate at the Lyon's corner houses, where the food was adequate and good. All restaurant charges were government controlled and for 1 shilling and 9pence (10.5pence) or 2 shillings and 3 pence (13.5 pence), an adequate lunch could still be had. The major restaurants or hotels were restricted to a maximum of 5 shillings (25 pence). There were no 'a la carte' menus, but if you bought a bottle of wine, you were well hammered. Carrots always accompanied your food, in view of its 'night vision' properties, and during my one year in London, whale steaks were on the menu as a good source of protein. Whale steaks were tasteless, tough and had the rubber consistency of a squash ball: once tasted, never again.

My entertainment in London varied quite a bit from my recent past, for war had intervened in-between. I now had to pay for everything. I was older, and loaded with testosterone. I continued with my boating in the Serpentine; skating at the Queen's Ice Rink; walking; running and sightseeing. I had bought a second-hand Voightlander camera from a serviceman, who no doubt, had obtained it in Germany, as part of war-booty. Compared with my Kodak box camera, this was marvellous. With it, I photographed a devastated London and the pictures were all perfect. Unfortunately, once whilst asleep on an L.M.S. train, the camera and the suitcase containing these photographs were stolen.

As I had boxed for Stonyhurst, I joined the Regent Street Polytechnic Boxing Club. Willie had won several boxing blues at Oxford. I believed I could follow in his footsteps. It was not to be. Two men, one an ex-commando, both heavier and older than me, were selected to box this 17-year old 'public school boy'. No respite in a four minute contest, with 2 minutes for each of my opponents, was a little too much for me to bear, even though I withstood their onslaught. For the next two weeks, I suffered from headaches and dizziness, and I knew that boxing for me as a sport was now over.

London Digs

My first London digs was at 39 Clanricarde Gardens. The people there, unlike in the north, were most unfriendly. Hardly a word was exchanged by the thirty or so residents, gracing its breakfast room. Silence was golden but boring: not even 'Good morning' was heard during my three months residential stay. Willie, however, was far more active and found a small faltlet in 11 Courtfield Gardens. His attempt to convince me to join him failed initially but then I joined him in April 1947. The flatlets there were vastly superior to any others I had seen and I became the paying guest of Geoffrey and Billie Parker. In 1963, Willie convinced them to settle in Torremolinos, a small, primitive and beautiful village, in the budding Costa del Sol.

Whilst the theatre was very much part of our pre-war London nightlife, post-war was very different. I had to pay for my tickets. In 1943, I had enjoyed Arthur Askey's antics in a Preston theatre. He was undoubtedly the best English comedian I was ever to see. He brought happiness and laughter to the audience and in the case of my Uncle Tuto, Peter and me, a very long walk from Preston to Longbridge. We were so enthralled by his antics, jokes and encores, that we left the Preston Theatre late. We missed our last bus home. There were no taxis. A long walk from Preston to Longridge was all that was needed, and with the blackout conditions prevailing, we were un-prepared for our night's ordeal. Carrots galore were in our home staple diet and it had been medically confirmed that they would help us see better at night. They did not. Several hours later, in the early hours of the morning, we arrived home. Poor old Uncle Tuto took the brunt of our scolding.

As I had seen a few musical shows in Lancashire, I convinced a fellow medical student to see this one in London's West End. At this show, a member of the audience was invited to the stage to engage one of the actors, in a game of table-tennis. The winning prize: "a dinner date with one of London's most dazzling, curvaceous blondes,—the main actress of the show". I had seen this act before. It was always a 'Put-up job' except on this occasion. Before the 'Put-up' person could get up, I was on my way to the stage. It was not long before I realized that my opponent was no match. Between the two of us, we had enough money, to take her to Lyon's Corner House, for a 2 shilling and three pence dinner and a shandy. It was difficult to lose but I managed it.

Troopships

Travelling from Gibraltar to England was not difficult, as my father was able to arrange transport. The cost of flying was several times more expensive than going by sea. A single air fare cost £100 and some more. Most of the ships returning to England were troopships or pre-war converted liners. This form of transport lasted a few years. You could acquire a passage on sufferance and you were "expected" to follow troopship discipline. Whilst my father paid for First Class accommodation (the only class for civilians), we all slept in a large dormitory. (There were no female students on these ships.) At 7 am the deafening wake up bell rang throughout the trooper. A hot salt-water shower was available, if there was no queue, but breakfast was at 8am sharp, and if you arrived late, lunch was your next meal. Life-boat drill was compulsory, and a daily ritual. Life-jackets had to be carried or worn, in the event of a loose mine hitting our hull. On two occasions we saw life-jackets floating, but did not stop. Evening meals were early and by 10 p.m., it was off to bed and lights out. Silence was enforced. Entertainment was provided by the soldiers during their morning P.T. exercises. Those of us, who had lived in England and knew what rationing was all about came prepared with loads of sweets and other items, not available or rationed in the U.K.

The U.K. Customs

The most unpleasant part of the troopship's 'cruise' was the return to its home-port, Southampton or Tilbury. Invariably, grey skies, rain and loud-mouthed seagulls greeted us. But it was the Customs Officers' behaviour that irked me most. Troops returning from the Middle and Far East, who had served Britain well, were searched excessively and made to pay for all items listed on a card. I kept to the rules throughout my life, except on one occasion.

In the late forties, Tangier was the Mecca of pre-war European civilisation. It was unscathed by war, and provided you were European, a very good life was there to be had. My father had given me £10 during one of my holidays to see Tangier.

Whilst there, I soon realised that I could make money in the Kasbah due to the unstable exchange rates. I was able to convert

£10 into a week's holiday (hotel and food included), three new watches and return home with £5 in hand. I could sell the watches easily in the United Kingdom. But the problem was how to smuggle them in. Prior to the landing at Southampton, I thought of a 'brilliant' idea. Two of the watches I would tie into the lower gaps of my groin and the other near my rear end. They felt reasonably comfortable. A walk around the trooper's deck caused no problem. From the upper deck, I could see the long custom's tables where every suitcase was opened, with many servicemen made to pay for items with little value. But what I had not brought into the smuggler's equation was the steep gangway, from the liner to the quayside. Carrying my heavy suitcase, I slipped. The rear end watch misbehaved, causing excruciating pain. There was no way I could relieve this pain without lowering my trousers and that was out of the question for I was now ashore. My movements towards the customs' bench were tortoise in speed and my facial expressions were consistent with considerable anal pain. A gentlemanly customs officer noticed my gait and facial expression. "You must have piles. I had mine operated last month and I know what it feels like. If you have nothing to declare, I will help you to the train". I could hardly show him the goods, unless I was prepared to lower my pants. So with a slow walk and a grimace my suitcase was carried by this good Samaritan to the train: slowly but surely. Following a heartfelt thank you, I walked to the train's toilet, and removed the offending watches: with immediate relief. Two nights later, at Wembley's greyhound stadium, I sold the watches to three bookmakers. They were very happy, for in the late forties, good watches were un-obtainable in the U.K. The pain was worth the profit but only just.

Summer Holidays 1945-53 R.G.Y.C.

As a medical student (1947-53) and later as a practising Gibraltarian doctor (1953-56), my visits to Gibraltar were restricted to one a year, and always, for the month of July or August. I was a member of the Royal Gibraltar Yacht Club (R.G.Y.C.) and during my vacation, I spent most of my time swimming in the sea or sailing in the bay. My sister Lennie's 'sharpie' 'Poor Fish' was put at my disposal for that month. I had many good sailing competitors in Louis Triay, Julio and Louis Fava, but invariably the winner was Charlie Bassadone. I kept a close eye on all of them, for I invariably was placed near the rear. The R.G.Y.C. was undoubtedly Gibraltar's five star club and all rules were strictly observed. The higher echelons of the military, civilians and their children formed most of its members. Young unmarried military and naval officers were also enrolled. No member could enter the club house's bar without a tie. Safarino, a Spaniard, served excellent lunches and dinner and in the summer evening drinks were served on 'The Hard'. The Benny (Benrimoj) brothers looked after the bar for years, and were known to many satisfied yachting generations.

The sunset gun, fired from the King's Bastion, was within 75 metres and directly above the club's roof. It gave a deafening sound even to those prepared for its thunder. As the gun fired, all the members on 'The Hard' stood up, and faced the flag as it was lowered, with those in uniform saluting. All flags in the fortress were lowered at sunset. There was no skylarking permitted on 'The Hard' and children were not allowed in after a certain time and then only in a restricted area. However one young officer, in his belief that he could push his selected civilian fully clothed into the sea, was particularly childish, since the civilian was me. I believed, at that time, in the philosophy of an eye for an eye. Afraid of my reaction, he fled, but only to return two weeks later in full military wear, prior to his regimental mess night. He believed, quite wrongly, that wearing the King's uniform and badge, he was safe. Despite his protestations, including that I was insulting the King's uniform, by lifting him, sword and all, I carried him to the exact spot, where he had pushed me in and I dumped him into the sea. Whether he complained to his C.O. or not, I never found out, but he was never seen again in the club.

Many servicemen were inclined to believe or made to believe, that here, they were a few pegs above the civilians. It was locally acceptable to many. There were three cinemas in Gibraltar: the Theatre Royal; the Rialto Cinema and the Naval Trust. The former two were owned by the Massias, an old established Jewish family with very high standards of professionalism and ethics. For them as indeed throughout Gibraltar's commercial businesses, the same rules applied, be they civilian or servicemen. In the Naval Trust Cinema, priority was given to the servicemen, and once the services' queue had ended, the Gibraltarians were allowed to buy the remaining seats and when necessary, a new queue formed. By 1945, the era in which Gibraltarians raised their hats and gave priority to the uniformed officers on our narrow pavements, was all but gone. I never saw this in England.

Cars

Whilst there were shortages of virtually everything in the U.K. there were none in Gibraltar, except for cars. From the time one ordered an 'export' car, to its delivery, it might have taken 3-6 months. It depended on U.K. industrial relations, which in the post-war period were exceptionally bad. Cars that were locally registered for six months could be re-exported to Spain for a higher price, since there was a great demand for second hand cars across the border. The importation of second hand cars, not new ones, was legal in Spain and as a result, many of the new cars sold here, had a resale proviso in some of the agents' earlier agreements. The only cars seen on Spanish roads were the 'G' registrations and the Spanish P.M.M. and E.T.T. The latter two, were the registration letters for government officials and in Spanish were dubbed para mi mujer (P.M.M.) (for my wife) and es te tambien, (E.T.T.) (and this one as well|). The roads were free from traffic and one could travel as fast as one would wish, even though the roads could hardly fit two cars, sideways. I broke my speed record on the Algeciras' straight mile, when I reached 50 M.P.H. Vibrations at the steering wheel of my 'Standard' car meant I had to reduce my speed to 40 M.P.H. for safe driving. The balanced wheel had not yet made its technological mark.

Spanish Customs

At the Spanish Customs, everyone crossing the border was searched: both ways. It looked good. It was when leaving Spain where the search was at its best. I overcame their excessive customs' zeal when entering, by having a lighted cigarette between my lips. I was a non-smoker. Following the examination of my car, I offered as a matter of courtesy, a cigarette from the newly opened packet. If he accepted, I followed it through more aggressively. "Do you want the packet?" The answer was always 'Si'. I never smuggled anything into Spain but this gesture gave me the same fast track entry, as was given to those with the 'red' pass, that V.I.P.'s had. It was on leaving Spain where the search was at its best. Fresh fruit, vegetables and eggs were as Spanish exports, 'verboten'. The car boot could never be filled to its potential, as confiscation of its contents was nearly guaranteed. The reason when given by the Guardia Civil was that by buying such groceries, one was depriving the Spanish poor and hungry of a good meal. It was utter nonsense, but to have said so, would have placed one in police custody.

The best way I could find to help these poor people was to fill my pockets with 1 and 5 peseta pieces and give to all that begged. By the time I reached Gibraltar, my pockets were empty, as the number in dire straits was considerable. Our smuggling consisted of farm produce and fruit. Most of it lay behind the legs of the long skirted back-seat passengers. The Guardia Civil would not have examined that area. A certain amount was in the car-boot for psychological reasons, as no woman returning from a day's outing, would have crossed the border empty-handed. At Gibraltar there were no restrictions, as to food importation.

The Spanish daily cleaners and domestic workers were bodily thin on crossing our border and excessively fat on their departure. Their extra large bloomers, bras and skirts contained many internal pockets, in which sugar, coffee, tea, butter and other essentials were transported every day, not only to La Liñea, but by Spanish workers crossing to Algeciras by ferry. Most of these items were unobtainable there or were poor in quality. Spanish exit chits were restricted to one crossing per day. Most of the food imported was for their own consumption or close relatives. However, if caught, a nod and a few Spanish pesetas paid to the Matronas (women customs officers), often did the trick for these imports were illegal. In some instances, the goods were confiscated and partially kept for the personal use of the Matronas. Generally speaking the domestics and other workers achieved their objective. With the male workers, tobacco smuggling was usually their preference. Anything over a used packet of 20 was confiscated. The tobacco in Gibraltar was not only cheaper but of better quality. Few carried more than one packet in their pocket, for all were body searched at La Liñea's customs post on their return home.

The big-time tobacco smugglers were the British and Spanish administrations, who accepted this state of affairs with their eyes wide open. The Gibraltar customs sheds were huge and contained billions of cigarettes, and a sea of alcohol. Selected exporters carried this ware 'legally' to importers, mostly in the North East of Spain or Majorca. The 'big' companies that directly exported their tobacco to Gibraltar were mainly British and American. They must have known prior to their exportation that Gibraltarians including the newly born could not have chain smoked 150 cigarettes or more per minute that was often bandied about. Other items, unobtainable in Spain, made their way though this territory. It was a case of "It takes two to tango". No drugs were locally exported, as the revenue and other government officers, would have made short shrift of the exporters.

Costa del Sol

The Costa del Sol developed and grew as a result of an influx of Gibraltarians and Britons wishing to settle there after the war.

Virtually, the whole of Europe was in devastation and countries like Portugal and Spain were mired with a dictator and poverty. With strict financial restrictions on all Britons (£10 on leaving the U.K.) and with Gibraltar's frontier legally free to export your U.K. wealth, the Costa del Sol began to take root. A new British colony on Spanish soil began to develop. With time, other nationals joined in. It was to the Gibraltarians, Britons, our airport, the U.K. and local bankers that the Costa del Sol owes its early development.

Marbella

In the 50's, Marbella's beaches were blackened with coal dust from its adjoining mine and the only tan available was a coal black one. Many therefore avoided its beaches. But as Franco loosened his grip, many hotels began to spring up along this beautiful coast. In the late 40's, there were more Brits enjoying its sun-drenched beaches than all other non-Spanish nationals put together.

Yet for me and others, there was plenty else to do and see outside Gibraltar. Fairs, bull-fights and the odd trip to Malaga and Seville filled what was left in my pleasure schedule. It was also the time of romance, and the Reina Christina Hotel at Algeciras had all the necessary ingredients for precisely that. Dancing in its gardens, with a clear view of the 'Rock' on a full moon night, was not to be missed. But like Cinderella, midnight was the time to leave, for if you were a few minutes late at the frontier, you spent the night in no-man's land. A fine followed the next day for spending the night illegally, and needless to add a dressing down; not only by your parents, but by your partner's parents as well.

Returning Home 1947-55

After the war, travelling to Gibraltar became exceptionally difficult. I had a good personal relationship with a few of the travel agents, who were in the process of establishing themselves. They knew that whatever was offered, I would accept, provided the sailing or flying departure time was more than 24 hours, from receiving their call. It always was, but only by another 12. The 10 hour night travelling from Dublin to London (1947-53) was easy. There was always plenty of room on the Dun Laoghaire ferry and boat train. Delays on this route were rare. Trunk calls to inform my parents of my arrival time were best avoided due to the 2-3 hour delays encountered in connecting with the receiver. Telegrams were better. In 1959, the first trunk call from a public telephone in Britain could be made without the need of an operator to connect you!

Generally speaking, air travel was best and easiest. The flight path from Northolt was Bordeaux-Lisbon-Gibraltar. The long delays in the primitive departure hall at Bordeaux often caused some friction between the passengers and air-carrier's staff. Fortunately for many, the Dakota was the only plane used to serve Gibraltar. It required frequent refuelling and had unintentional gliding properties. The airlines supplying this route were British European Airways (B.E.A.) and Hunting Clan. Flying over Spain was verboten by General Franco, so our flight path following Bordeaux was Lisbon, where we spent the night in the casino town of Estoril. Next morning, to Gibraltar via the Atlantic. As General Franco mellowed and his fears of a coup subsided, our flight path changed, refuelling at Bordeaux and Madrid. There was little to buy at either capitals, but in Lisbon (Estoril) there was a casino to tempt you. Post-war

U.K. currency restrictions (£10) for spending were strictly enforced at all U.K. exit points by customs.

Not long after the Madrid route had been opened to B.E.A. I suffered my first air crash at Madrid's Barajas airport (N 2). As you can tell, I survived. Our Dakota hit a runway obstacle on take off. We had full fuel tanks for the purpose of stopping in Madrid was precisely one of refuelling. The plane shuddered upon hitting the object, and seconds later we were on our way skywards. Sitting in the front seat, I saw the starboard wheel fall off and seconds later the propeller followed suit. We were a few hundred feet up and the only solution was now to crash. It did but some miles away, ending with a 45 ° nose starboard alignment. I helped the air-hostess with the passengers' evacuation via the rear of the plane. There was no fire or panic. When the fire fighters arrived at what appeared to be a long time later, I heard one of them say: "Thank God the plane has not caught fire, for there is no water in the tender's tank". We all stayed at the prestigious and beautiful Palace Hotel and the next day another plane arrived and flew us to Gibraltar. Ernest Guetta a Gibraltarian and Madrid resident, who was a very good friend of my father, loaned me 1000 pesetas. With that amount, the air-hostess and I saw Madrid. Over the years, planes technologically improved and landing at Bordeaux fortunately ended and years later, at Madrid. Our expenses were naturally paid by the airline, since it was them that had been at fault, but only to a point. The wine at dinner was on my account. During Franco's rule, obstacles were often left on the runway intentionally and at appropriate places. They were there to prevent 'enemy' planes from landing without permission.

There was no such thing as a computerised travelling booking system, and if my intention was to arrive at a particular place, I accepted whatever was on offer. On three occasions I was offered a way of travel that I would never experience again. The first was in December 1948 to attend my sister's wedding. I was offered a flight ticket from Herne Bay to Gibraltar on the morning of the 15, leaving on the evening of the next day. I left Dublin that same evening by boat and took the night train from Holyhead to London, arriving at Euston about 8 am. A good breakfast and then to Victoria's Sea-Bird House: the home of B.O.A.C. This impressive building was clean and architecturally modern. A few very well dressed transatlantic passengers, American and obviously well to do, walked in the sparsely filled hall (unlike today's airport lounges). Britain still had rationing, and the yanks stood out, when compared with the badly dressed nationals. The numbers waiting to fly to the U.S. were minimal. The R.M.S. Queen Elizabeth and Queen Mary and other transatlantic liners were in direct competition with B.O.A.C. The sea-trip to the U.S. was the 'in-thing' and flying was not.

Our departure time from Sea-Bird House was 8 pm and this was postponed to 11:30 p.m. We travelled by coach to Bournemouth. I wondered what the airport was like, and assumed incorrectly, that the name for Bournemouth's airport was Herne Bay. A few hours later the coach stopped by the quay-side. All the passengers were males and fit. They looked like servicemen. A boat awaited us. Before I knew where I was going, I found myself climbing onto a flying boat. I had no idea till I boarded the craft that I was flying to Gibraltar on a sea-plane, and on a military one, at that. The flight path took us over the Bay of Biscay, the Atlantic, and outside Franco's and Salazar's jurisdictions.

We landed in the Admiralty Harbour form north to south and tied up just west of the R.G.Y.C. As we took off at night, there was little to see. The daylight landing, next morning however, was fantastic and exhilarating. As the plane hit the water, we felt a big thump and were all suddenly propelled forwards. My view from the port-hole was temporarily obliterated by the massive splash and spray. As we quickly slowed down, the spray got less and within seconds, 'The Rock' came into view once again. Within minutes of our landing the plane was secured to one of the harbour's moorings and a few of us were taken by R.A.F. tender to the north side of Coaling Island. Once on land, I was told: "That's it". There was no passport or customs check. I walked home un-announced, as there was no way of letting my parents know of my arrival time. I arrived on time for my sister's wedding, but only just.

On another occasion, I was offered the liner Arcadia's stateroom, following a last minute cancellation by someone else. The ship was on its maiden voyage to Brazil and was calling at Lisbon. This was the nearest port to Gibraltar, if I wished to arrive there by a certain date. An ultra-reasonable price came with the offer and I could not refuse. I had four hours to pack and arrive at Dun Laoghiare. Twenty four hours to cross the Irish Sea; take the night train (express) from Holyhead to Euston station, and from there to London's Victoria for Southampton. I made it, but what never occurred to my young mind, was the fact that the liner was on its maiden voyage and all entertainment and drinks would be priced far above what I experienced as a student in Dublin.

As part of the stateroom's price tag, I had to vacate my luxurious quarters, several hours before the ship's arrival in Lisbon, for the stateroom had to be made 'clean and respectable' for the oncoming V.I.P. That was not a problem, but what was, were the drinks and other expenses onboard, which had left me £3 in pocket. I still had to get to Gibraltar and there were no credit cards at the time.

Once on shore, I searched for the Seville bus but failed to find it. I was, fortunate enough to meet two of Gibraltar's great Samaritans: Mariola and Adolfo Russo. Without telling them of my financial plight, Adolfo offered me a lift to Gibraltar the next day. I stayed with them in their Lisbon and Seville hotels, wined and dined and at no cost to me. I enjoyed their company immensely. I was lucky for had I not met them, my trip would have been tough, very tough.

And my third travel agent's offer that I remembered well was on a Spanish plane. I had booked form London to Madrid via San Sebastian. The plane left London full, but for reasons unknown and unexplained to the passengers, the flight ended at San Sebastian. Despite protestations, we were ignored but after several hours, the authorities finally took heed, and placed at our disposal a small plane.

The 'new' plane was a ten-seater. It had one pilot and no navigator. There was one seat on each side of the aisle, and one port-hole per passenger. All passengers had a good view of the pilot (and his view) since there was no partition curtain to separate us. We flew below the clouds and followed what appeared to be the Madrid road. There were not many roads below, so our navigation was not as difficult as it might have been in a more sophisticated country. There were ten passengers onboard. It was very interesting to see the Spanish countryside from only a few thousand feet up and below the clouds.

Unfortunately I had an American middle-aged woman on the other side of the aisle, who was in the early stages of hysteria. She could not look out of her window nor look at the pilot. "What happens, if he flies into a cloud and gets lost?" "What happens if he gets a heart attack?" Whilst the answers were obvious, I could not tell her. "May I hold your hand" she said "as I am very nervous?" As I took her hand, I thought, "You're not the only one".

Most Americans in Europe read the New York Herald Tribune, and all at one time or another, must have seen the Spanish tourist agency full page advert. "Spain is different". On this flight she was made fully aware of this fact.

Chapter 7

TRINITY COLLEGE, DUBLIN 1947-53

The Early Days

Leaving London's Euston station for Holyhead was not as easy as one would expect, for the night train was always packed. As I had arrived early, I was able to have the window seat, in a compartment fit for 8. The L.M.S. (London Midland and Scottish) train left on time. After an exhausting journey, the train arrived in Holyhead on time, at 2.30 a.m. After customs' clearance, I boarded the ferry for Kingston, Ireland, later renamed Dun Laoghaire. Although the month was October the Irish Sea behaved well and was calm. It was early dawn when the gentle hills of Kingston, Howth and Dublin came into view. The panorama was superb and the sky, free from clouds. The Irish customs' officers were more like the Gibraltarians, ready to help and extremely courteous. Within minutes, I was on my way to board the train for Westland Row, one of Dublin's railway stations. The train, as compared with Britain, was less comfortable and modern. As we chugged along, I realised that speed was not an essential part of the Irish railway system, but fortunately it allowed me, to see the stunning scenic views of the bay from Kingston, Blackrock and then Sandymount. Like everything in life, my first impressions were soon marred, as we approached the inner Dublin slums. Further shocks were to follow in quick succession. I had arrived at a time of industrial unrest, and what was worse, unknown to me. At Westland Row, there were no taxis to be seen, only horse-drawn cabbies. I had been on one in Gibraltar, so why not in Dublin? I hopped up and asked the cab-driver to take me to a first class hotel but not a luxury one. "I know just the place for you" and drove onto Pearse Street. Shortly after, he bent over to tell me that we were "passing Trinity College". This side of Trinity, well carbonised, is not its best view, either then or now: another shock. As we crossed O'Connell Bridge into O'Connell Street he muttered something which I could not understand. It was probably about O'Connell's Statue. But his voice became loud and clear, as we passed the post office. "On your right is Nelsons Pillar—the only famous military man, not to have been Irish". Was he right, I asked myself: Montgomery, Alexander and Wellington were all Irish, but I was too busy looking outwardly, as to decide whether he was right or wrong. Within another five minutes, the cab stopped. "This is your hotel: the Belvedere".

I was now about to have another problem with the receptionist, as to my marital status. I could neither have a single or a double room, because I was not married! I had to share a room, and needless to add, with a man: a woman would have been better. I was confused, but accepted as all I wanted was to lie down for a few hours' rest. After I woke, I headed for Trinity College to register.

O'Connell Street was like the start of the 'Tour de France' with cyclists everywhere; no buses, no trams and few cars. Westmoreland

Street was the same. To add insult to injury, it was raining; soft rain as the Irish call it. It wets! Like Oxford and other European cities, buildings like Trinity and the Bank of Ireland, on the opposite side of College Green, were well carbonised. This was the era of severe pollution: fog and smog were still with their inhabitants. Clean air was not yet a political issue. Dublin roads, like those seen in London's Hyde Park Corner, were paved with wooden blocks, and as such when wet, were very slippery. The Irish police performed miracles in controlling the hordes of cyclists, who charged when given the go-ahead signal.

At 12.30 p.m. I arrived at what was to be the Gates of Heaven for the next six years: Trinity's front gate (P 2). Courteous porters directed me to the Admissions Office, where registration was required with the appropriate fees. There was a queue, but not long. In this line up, the age group varied considerably, due to the effects of war. Captain Shaw, the Admissions Officer, a gentleman, small and white-haired, who insisted on being addressed properly. I knew how to address Captain Tobin and others at Stonyhurst, so I had no problem. But the student two ahead of me obviously had. He was about ten or more years older than me. "Young man, you address me as Captain Shaw or Sir, not as Mr Shaw. Now, what is your name?" "I am Colonel . . . . " He had recently been demobbed from the British army.

I could not pay my admission fees, even though I had a cheque payable to me, waiting to be lodged. The banks were also on strike, so the only money I had, was my travelling money, which I required for food and accommodation.

At the Admissions Office, they were very helpful, but first the secretary suggested I go for a meal to the Dining Hall, a further

100 metres across The Square (P 20). The Dining Hall was similar to Stonyhurst, except the ceiling was much higher and the hall much larger. Unlike Stonyhurst, whose walls were graced with the paintings of its seven Victoria Crosses, and Cardinal Vaughan, this hall held its famous alumni and benefactors. The paintings were much larger as befitted the size of the hall. Away from the main door, in a large corner, lay a self-service counter for the male Undergraduates, managed by the Lady Superintendent of the kitchens. She was medium-sized, white-haired, about 50 years old and acted more like a mother, than a superintendent. The quantity, quality and choice of foods were more in keeping with Hollywood and the cost was ultra-reasonable. It could not be bettered. She advised most students, what she considered was best on that day. I always accepted her advice, and left the Dining Hall very satisfied.

With no public transport functioning, the banks closed, taxis unavailable, and no digs, I was in a bad way. But the Admissions Officer came my way again, for after lunch, I got fixed up with accommodation at Park Avenue One, Sandymount (P 5). A private car would collect me from the hotel at 9.30 a.m. the next day. I now had a roof over my head, but to walk nearly four miles to College before my lectures was not a good idea. A bike had to be bought if I was to avoid long walks on a regular basis, for there appeared to be no end to the transport strike.

A long walk to Dorset Street and its surrounding areas, led me to Blair's cycle shop. This area lay in a deprived part of Dublin. Blair needed customers, and I needed a bicycle but did not have the ready cash to pay for one. With a shortage of bicycles for sale throughout Dublin, and with post-war British exports not able to cope with Irish demand, my prospects were dim. But with the luck of Blair and his friends, he was soon able to supply me with one. He was so good and obliging that I continued using his shop during the whole of my stay in Dublin. Later on, I motorised my cycle, until Vespas came to the market and his shop. His service was prompt and excellent. Years later, as a doctor, I returned to his shop, but he was no longer there. I tried without luck to trace him. He was gone.

Phone calls to Gibraltar, either from London or Dublin could take three or more hours before you were connected. Telephone booths were out, unless you were prepared to take on, physically, the awaiting callers. I was not. Calls were therefore made from the General Post Office where one or two newspapers could be read, whilst waiting. Finally the strike came to an end. The Bank of Ireland, across College Green, obliged and I opened my account there. My first payment was to Trinity.

Park Avenue One in Sandymount (P 5) was my comfortable digs for the next three months, with evening meals included. The Irish tea consisted of eggs, bacon, sausages, black pudding and chips, with once a week, a steak. Fish was served on Friday evening. My room had a view of a well-cared garden. It could not have been bettered. And in the first three months, I cycled to the medical school for 9 a.m. lectures. All lectures started on time and if you were late, you stayed out. You would be refused entry.

With Blair's help and normality returning to Dublin after the strikes, my new bicycle opened the Dublin world to me. It took me a good 20 minutes to get to Trinity. Provided you accepted two essential road rules, you could avoid your premature obituary paragraph: "Drive carefully on rainy days especially if there are tram-lines in your wheels vicinity, and beware of old roads made with wooden blocks." I once had the experience of London's Hyde Park Corner, on a rainy day, when our car skidded on the wooden blocks and came face to face with an oncoming police car. Our driver sped off and we were saved from an embarrassing situation with the police. As to the former, I had come down in the first two weeks of cycle ownership. Tram lines on the same level as the road are dangerous.

Lectures

Medical students had to attend 90 per cent of lectures and simple checks were made prior to the lecture starting. Those whose head and neck, when seated, did not cover their number, were marked as absent. The lectures were so interesting, that to have missed one, would have been a great pity. So I missed none. There was one lecturer who towered above the rest. He was Ernest Walton, Professor of Physics. He along with Sir John Cockcroft, at Cambridge University had won the Nobel Prize in Physics on the "transmutation of atomic nuclei by artificially accelerated atomic particles". In simple language, he had split the atom. It was said, whether factual or not, that he had refused to work with the team that created the atom bomb. His work was for peaceful purposes. He was not prepared to use his knowledge in the destruction of mankind, as the atom bomb might well do in the future.

Mortal Sin

Before I left Gibraltar for Dublin, members of my paternal family, with the help of Sister Patricia, a nun from Liverpool, had suggested that University College, Dublin was the better of the two universities. 'It was Catholic'. I had no intention of crossing the 'Rubicon'. To this end, Bishop Fitzgerald, a good friend of the family, and as Irish, as the best in Ireland can be, gave me a letter which I had to give personally to Dublin's Archbishop Dr McQuaid on my arrival. What the letter contained, I never found out, but after being kept waiting for one hour, at the Bishop's Palace, he declined to see me. The letter was then handed to the secretary and I left. It wasn't long before I knew the reason (P 9). Every Easter, the pastoral letter from Dr McQuaid contained reference to Trinity College . . . . 'Under the pain of Mortal Sin no Catholic can attend the Protestant University of Trinity College, Dublin'. The same reasoning would have applied to Trinity in Cambridge or Oxford, since their founder was also Queen Elizabeth. There was no Catholic ban in England. Most of the Catholic students accepted to Trinity attended Mass at Clarendon Street, and most of us received Holy Communion. To attend a Jesuit school gave one a good Catholic foundation for life. In Andalucía, Southern Spain, Cardinal Segura had banned dancing, in all its forms, as immoral and sinful; yet the same rule, fortunately, was not in force in Dublin. Had it been it would most certainly have been ignored, for I could not have believed, that the happy and carefree Irish would have accepted such Puritanism. In Andalucía, it was mainly ignored. I certainly did!

Franco's police were always on the look-out to teach morality, especially to those who abided by the law. My brother and I, during our Easter holidays, had gone to Cadiz, by the only means of transport available to those without a driving licence—a bus. The Atlantic beach of Cadiz is not only big, but beautiful. The tides keep it clean. On our first and last day to be, we went to the beach. We were semi-arrested for insulting the ladies of Cadiz, by walking on the beach: topless. Whilst my pre-war bathing costume covered all, my post-war one did not. The style in Britain had changed during the war to bathing trunks. It covered from the belly-button to below the knees. Our chest was exposed. That was the offence. It was a most serious and offensive crime and an insult to the Spanish women on the beach. The beach was like a desert, for it was early April and few Spaniards would have been on its sands, since the official bathing season was some months away. We paid the exorbitant fine of 1000 pesetas and obtained an 'official receipt'. The money, no doubt a perk, helped the Guardia, with his monthly expenses. We had no choice for it was a question of 'pay up or come to the police station'. We paid up and prematurely returned to Gibraltar, where religious sanity prevailed, and our remaining pesetas could be put to better use.

Rathfarnham Abbey and the Graduates Memorial Building (G.M.B.)

Prior to my departure for Ireland, my mother had warned me of the dangers of the I.R.A. She suggested I see her very good friend and past teacher at Gibraltar's Loreto Convent, now resident in Rathfarnham Abbey, Dublin. Within weeks of my arrival, I called at the convent and saw Mother Gonzales. My visit turned into a monthly one. On my second visit, I also met Mother Gabriel Clarke, who also had worked in Gibraltar. Tea and cakes and a ninety minute visit was appreciated by all. This continued until their deaths, some years later. But during our conversations, Mother Gabriel Clarke, mentioned that she knew Sir Thomas Moloney, the

Vice-Chancellor of Trinity. "I know Sir Thomas Moloney well", she said and "I see him frequently. Would you like to live in Trinity? I can ask him, but I cannot guarantee any success".

Just before Christmas, the rooms on the second floor of Number 28, in the Graduates Memorial Building (G.M.B.) in Trinity became vacant. I was offered the rooms and immediately accepted. The front part of the flat consisted of a sitting room, kitchen and a small corridor. It faced Front Square (P 2 & P3). On the other side of the communal landing lay my bedroom and a small room for coal. It faced Botany Bay. There was no central heating or running water. There was one communal toilet and one water tap for the five students who graced its floor. The bathroom was in another building and you were restricted to one weekly. But showers, following sport or exercise, were available at the College's sports pavilion, any time of day.

The lecture rooms were now much closer and the pre-med subjects of botany, zoology, physics and chemistry, could be attended to, without arriving in a rain-soaked state. Breakfast consisted of a cup of coffee. The good breakfast at Park Avenue was permanently out. I was now at the centre of University life, not at its periphery. I joined the University Philosophical Society, but unfortunately missed many of its debates and famous speakers. It was a good place to meet non-medical students.

My Early Friends

I had met in my first Michaelmas Term, the beautiful Deirdre Mulcahy (P 27 sitting 2nd Lt), as a result of my Stonyhurst connections. She invited me to her house in Aylesbury Road during my first Christmas in Dublin. But it was in the vicinity of Trinity, to the many coffee shops surrounding the University, that within a short time, I had met many non-medical students and others. Dublin was a very friendly city. Living in Trinity was bliss. It had rules as you would expect in any college (P 11, 12, 14, 15). They were not draconian: a halfway house between Pembroke College, Oxford and Stonyhurst.

At Roberts Café I met man about town, Michael Drummond who knew Dublin well, just before Christmas. In my first year, he introduced me to one of the Noyek's and as a result was invited to my first Christmas party in Kingston. I had to leave early, so as to make it back on time to Trinity. Gates closed at 11 p.m. Unfortunately, I missed the last tram, and a long walk awaited me, leading me to arrive somewhat late at the Front Gate of the College. There was no scolding, but only a smile, a laugh and a talk. The world of university socialising had begun but not on Christmas or Boxing Day. Unable to return to Gibraltar as a result of the short term and lack of transport, I remained in Dublin. Christmas and Boxing Day 1947 was the loneliest I ever experienced, for I was totally unprepared. Dublin was more like a ghost town than a bustling city. Believing that hotels and restaurants would be open to serve Christmas lunch was correct, but only for those who had booked and in some cases weeks earlier. There was 'no room in any inn', and my Christmas lunch consisted of stale bread, marmalade and water. The 48 hours was quickly over. The next Christmas was spent in Gibraltar, for my sister's wedding, and the following year with my brother Willie at Killarney. By the end of the Christmas' holidays 1947, I had established a good friendship with Michael Drummond, who then became my premier introducer to the fair city and its fair ladies.

Socialising in my second term became possible, as I no longer had to endure rain soaked cycles to and from Sandymount. What better people to share my time than with my year's hard working medical students in coffee shops. I enjoyed the company of Barbara Cooke, Monica Taylor, Ouida D'Abreu, Beulah Knox, Mary Heaf, Margaret McMullan and a host of others, too numerous to mention, during those very short years of study. When I met them once again, 50 years later, none had changed other than for the silvery hair, associated with experience and time. Dr Beulah Knox (later Bewley) had the distinction of being honoured with a D.B.E.—Dame Beulah Bewley. Soon after entering College, I met the men who in later life would outshine professionally in their academia: Jimmie Milliken, Ian Bailey (P 24, P28), Ernest Weyhausen, Paris Panayottou (P19 4 right), Paul Osterberg (P 22), Billy Brownlees and a host of others. It was with the first four that my life became medically and socially entwined.

The Pre-med and Sneezing

Pre-med was a hard year, and academically only a percentage of us would pass. I had to pass, if my wish to be a doctor would come to fruition. I had to pass it at the first go, as otherwise there would be no summer holidays in Gibraltar. I had an enormous obstacle to overcome, with the soft Irish rain and its resulting luscious green fields. I was plagued, from a very early age, with hay fever, and the result was uncontrollable sneezing and severe allergic conjunctivitis. Studying in late spring and early summer was exceptionally difficult, partly as the result of my allergy to Timothy Grass, and partly to the drowsing effects of 25 mgms of

Phenergan thrice daily. (The only tablets available). The antidote was large amounts of caffeinated coffee, Kleenex and abundance of handkerchiefs. I often prayed, though unsuccessfully, that my examinations would take place during the Michaelmas or Easter term, when those with allergies could contest the examinations on a level playing field. It was not to be. Rain was always welcomed and fortunately there was plenty around. A few years later, the great Dr Heber McMahon of Sir Patrick Dun's Hospital, suggested a skin scratch test for Timothy Grass, as he was convinced my allergy could be cured. Within minutes of the test, I had an anaphylactic reaction requiring emergency resuscitation. The treatment was abandoned. From now on I had to 'sneeze and bear it'. Having passed, at the first go, and having enjoyed my last carefree Gibraltar holiday, I was now ready for the first M.B. (Bachelor of Medicine) course.

TRINITY COLLEGE, DUBLIN.

P.

Aeriel View.

Front Gate.

The library.
(Real Ireland design).

Rubric Building *(by Brian Power).*

The square. *(Real Ireland design).*

P.

Pre-Med *(1947)*.
Monica Taylor, Cecil Isola and Barbara Cooke.

Loreto Abbey. Rathfarnham, Dublin.

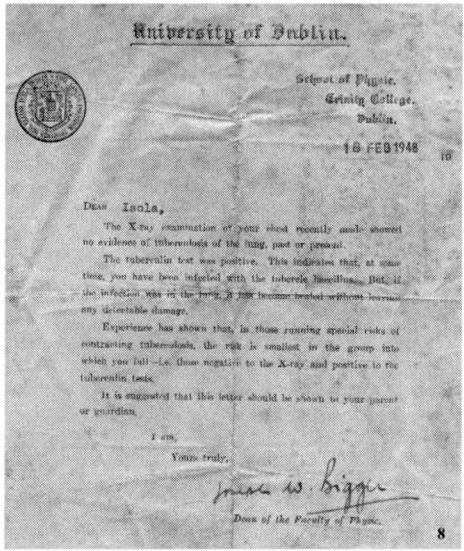

Sandymount:
1. Railway crossing and station.
2. Train. *(1947 model)*.
3. Park Avenue.

Doctors to be! *(November 1947)*.
Westmoreland St.
Cecil Isola and Jimmie Milliken.

"They cared".

Our Catholics and the Ban
November 27th, 1969

The illegal immigrants into Trinity are still struggling for legitimacy. The Laurentian Society was founded in 1953 as a social society for the 200 odd Roman Catholics attending Trinity. Now the number of Catholics has increased to over a third of the student body, and the Laurentian Society has undergone a complete change to accommodate the increasing numbers of Catholics, and to cope with the problems created by the still existing, still enforced ban on Irish Catholics studying in T.C.D.

The first statement banning Irish Roman Catholics from Trinity, contained in the Maynooth Statutes of 1955, has been stringently enforced by Dr. John Charles McQuaid, who became Archbishop of Dublin in 1944.

The ban states that Catholics commit a grave sin of disobedience if they attend a non-Catholic University, as the latter represents a grave danger to their faith and morals.

What it means, in effect, is that Roman Catholics entering Trinity College without the permission of the Hierarchy are « living in sin. »

Therefore, as they are not supposed to attend Trinity, Irish Catholics are actually ignored by the Hierarchy. According to Gus Mac Amhlaigh, the Chairman of the Society, their immediate aim is to gain recognition by the Hierarchy of the Irish Roman Catholics and to receive a resident Roman Catholic Dean. He, on behalf of the Society, engaged in frequent correspondence with the relevant authority on this subject, but has received an uncompromising answer at the moment « No. »

From a T.C.D. pamphlet signed Sheena Crummie.

Irish Squash Championships
He was so old (32 years) that I decide to give him a chance. He whacked me! Out first round.

Formal regulations are easily complied with, and in accepting rooms from the Provost you bind yourself to obey them. If you observe the regulations regularly you will avoid unnecessary trouble both for yourself and for me. If you are a member of the Church of Ireland or of the Church of England you must attend service in the College Chapel on Sunday mornings wearing a surplice. At present it may not be easy to obtain a surplice, and if you have not been able to get one you may sit in the gallery after you have handed an attendance card to the Marker in the usual way. Other students while in residence must attend the service of whatever Church they belong to, and I am authorized to require any student to produce to me a certificate from the proper authority showing that he has attended services regularly.

College rules for residents.

In your rooms you will be looked after by your "Skip." You will find your Skip anxious to do his best, but you must remember that he probably has fourteen other students to look after besides yourself, and by a little thought you can avoid creating unnecessary work for him. As Sunday is your holiday, remember that the Skip hopes that it will be his holiday also, and if you do not get up at a reasonable hour you cannot expect the Skip to wait all morning until you choose to do so.

"They cared".

'IF A FEMALE HAD ONCE PASSED THE GATE ...

... it would be practically impossible to watch what buildings or what chambers she might enter, or how long she might remain there.'

Thus, in 1895, the Board of Trinity College wrote of the grave dangers which would face the College if women students were admitted onto the campus. However, by 1904 the Board had changed its mind and women students were admitted, but subject to restricting rules.

As many of you will remember, women students up to the 1960s had to leave College by 6pm and could only return to the Library or an evening meeting by signing themselves through Front Gate. Women students could not dine on Commons, could not join the major societies, and could not be elected Foundation Scholars. Similarly, female members of staff could not be members of the Common Room, dine on Commons or be elected to Fellowship. All this was to change in the late 1960s, and the College now has a woman Chancellor, a woman Vice-Provost, and women in many senior academic and administrative posts.

Opposition to the higher education of women was very strong a hundred years ago and TCD resisted all requests to admit women during the ten years prior to 1904. The admission of women to Trinity was a very important step forward in the development of co-education and higher education in Ireland.

Students may not entertain ladies in their rooms without my permission, and requests for permission, whether verbal or by letter, must reach me not later than the preceding day and the names and addresses of the ladies must be given. If the ladies are students of the College this must be stated and they must get permission from the Lady Registrar. Ladies must leave College by 6 p.m.

Ladies must leave College by 6 p.m.

All resident students except Graduates may be required to attend Night Roll during lecture term, but Scholars and Sophisters are usually excused. Senior Freshmen attend at least twice a week and Junior Freshmen at least three times a week. After Night Roll, which is called at 9 o'clock (except during Trinity Term when it is called at 10 o'clock), no Freshman (other than a Scholar) may leave College without special permission from the Provost or Junior Dean. Freshman Scholars and Junior Sophisters are allowed to leave College between the hours of 9 p.m. and 11 p.m. on a limited number of occasions. Senior Sophisters and Graduates are usually permitted to leave College between these hours. All students must return to College before mid-night unless they have received permission from the Junior Dean to return at a later hour. This rule is usually relaxed in the case of Senior Sophisters, Graduates and Scholars. Students attending a dance held by a College society or club need not obtain formal permission on such occasions.

Rules for residents.

PLEASURE. P.

Metropole, Dublin. *(1948)* Law and Commerce Dance. University College.

Gresham Hotel, Dublin. *(1950)*.
Clongowes Jubilee Dance.

Metropole, Dublin. *(1949)*.
21st Birthday.

Royal Hotel, Bray. *(1952)*.
May, 2nd from right. First dance with her.

"Old Boys" Dance at Kilcroney, Co. Wicklow

Former scholars of two famous English schools, Stonyhurst and Downside, gave their first ball in Ireland, at Kilcroney. Many came across the channel for the event, whose success will certainly ensure its repetition

At supper Mr. B. McKenna, of Trinity College, Dublin, was sitting with Miss Phyllis McMahon and Mr. Cecil Isola, formerly of Stonyhurst, who most efficiently organised the ball

The Tatler and Bystander.

STONYHURST AND DOWNSIDE BALL AT KILCRONEY

The idea of past pupils of these two leading English public schools holding a dance in this country was a charming one and brought to Kilcroney mostly young people—together at Kilcroney. It was more like a really gay private party than the usual past pupils' dance. Most of the credit for its organisation goes to undergraduates of Trinity and National and all went so well that it is hoped to make it an annual event. There were among the patron members of both schools. On the Stonyhurst side were Lt. Col. and Mrs. P. H. Considine; Mr. and Mrs. G. V. Maher; Major and Mrs. E. M. Murphy; Mr. and Mrs. J. J. O'Connor (whose party included their daughter Kitty who wore a very becoming gown of emerald taffeta; Mr. Harry Tunney; Miss Nora O'Connor and Mr. Arthur McDonald); and Professor and Mrs. T. T. O'Farrell. The Downside patrons included Col. and Mrs. Denis Daly; the Duc and Duchesse de Stacpoole; the Earl and Countess of Fingall; and Mr. and Mrs. Dan Levins Moore.

Seated near the band I saw Captain and the Hon. Mrs. Emmett's party from Altidore Castle. She looked very striking in a gown of palest orange chiffon. Their guests included their daughter and son-in-law, Mr. and Mrs. Corballis, Mr. R. Corballis and Miss Roma Smyth who returned from the U.S. some months ago. Miss Smyth's gown was of purple striped taffeta.

Others who had parties were Mr. and Mrs. H. Chester-Walshe; Mr. and Mrs. Tommy S. Martin (who were among the Downside patrons) had a party of four; Mr. John McGuire whose party of six included his attractive sister, Barbara, whose gown of pale mauve chiffon contrasted with her blonde hair; Mr. and Mrs. Harry Meade who went off early as they were planning to go down the country for Whit. Their party included their elder son Feilim who is at University College; Miss Paddy O'Sullivan wearing a gown of bronze and black brocade; Miss Maura Quigley—a visitor from Scotland—and Mr. Frank Kelly.

The honorary secretaries, Mr. Cecil Isola who is a medical student at Trinity, and Mr. Derek Martin both had parties of young people. For Mr. Isola it was really a celebration as the B.A. degree had been conferred on him the previous day. His party included Miss Grace O'Malley wearing black tulle; Miss Jean Robertson; Miss Una O'Friel wearing a gown of two-tone satin, and Mr. David Lindsay. In Mr. Martin's party I saw good looking Miss Oonagh Moran in a full-skirted gown of mauve satin, Miss Arlette Grew and her brother Jimmy.

Others enjoying this dinner ball (the dinner was really sumptuous) were Mr. and Mrs. J. R. C. Green—her brother is Mr. Jackman, V.C.; Mr. and Mrs. John Ronan who made the journey from Cork; Lt. Col. and Mrs. J. W. Place; Col. Purcell who hunts with the Bray Harriers and Mrs. Purcell in a gown of pearl grey

JUNE, 1951

Irish Tatler and Sketch.

TWO MORE PICTURES FROM THE DOWNSIDE AND STONYHURST JOINT REUNION

P.

L. to r., seated: Miss Jean Robertson, Mr. Evan Agnostoros, Miss Maura Fann, Mr. David Lindsay, Miss Audrey McNamara, and Mr. P. Peters. At back: Mr. Cecil Isola, Miss Rosemary Kelly, Dr. Alex Meldrum, Miss Patricia Plunkett, and Mr. Michael Drummond.

Downside—Stonyhurst Dance

Last month Downside and Stonyhurst Past Pupils once again combined to organise their second dinner-dance which this year was held in the Royal Hibernian Hotel. The function was very well attended and was one of the most enjoyable dances of Spring Show Week.

The Stonyhurst Treasurer, Mr. James Green brought a large party which included his wife, Mr. and Mrs. V. Maher, who live in County Wexford, and Mr. and Mrs. R. Tierney, the latter wearing a chic gown of black crepe.

Mr. David Fitzgerald, the Downside Treasurer was escorting his wife who wore a striking ballet-length gown of black and white striped taffeta. Also in this party were Mr. and Mrs. T. G. McVeagh, she wearing a lovely dress of grey tulle.

At another table one of Stonyhurst's Patrons and one of its greatest supporters—Mr. James O'Connor—was escorting his wife, who wore a smart gown of black crepe which was studded with sequins.

Mr. Cecil Isola, one of the hon. secs., who worked tirelessly for the success of the Dance was dancing with Miss Jean Robertson who looked lovely in a dress of yellow organdie. Other members of this gay party were Mr. John Fennell who was escorting Miss Cinnia Costello, Miss M. Jann, recently returned from Tanganyka and who was wearing a beautiful gown of gold moiré and another visitor to Ireland, Miss M. Ingram of Poona, India.

Another Committee member, Mr. Paddy Quigley, had a large party at his table which included Mr. Phelim Meade who was escorting Miss Clothilde Borga who looked lovely in a chic gown of grey slipper satin, Miss Iris Quin, Mr. Billy Lacy and Mr. Barry O'Reilly who was escorting Miss Angela Kelly who wore a bouffant dress of pink organdie.

Others whom I saw dancing were Mr. T. G. McElhinney and his fiancée, Miss Diana O'Gorman-Quin, who are to be married this month, Mr. Maurice Legear and Miss Maeve Pryce, Miss Annette O'Gorman-Quin and Mr. Kenneth Smith.

DOWNSIDE STONYHURST

DANCE
at
ROYAL HIBERNIAN HOTEL, DUBLIN
on
FRIDAY, 9th MAY, 1952

Social and Personal. (*May 1952*).

SIR PATRICK DUN'S RUGBY FOOTBALL CLUB
SEASON 1950/51

D. ELLIS, D. A. LANE, N. BOLAND, C. FAGAN, R. JEVERS, D. BARRETT, F. J. SCALES
P. OSTERBERG, W. PACKHAM, J. H. VAN HOFMEYR, T. E. WINCKWORTH (Captain), J. R. GILL, G. T. NELSON, R. J. WEIR
J. HYSLOP, C. ISOLA

SIR PATRICK DUN'S HOSPITAL

A Sir Patrick's Dun's forward breaking away in the semi-finals cup of the Hospital's Rugby Cup at Clonskeagh yesterday which St. Vincents won.
(Irish Times).

GRADUATION: THE BEGINNING.

Five Doctors to be. From L to R: Edna Murphy, Kay McWilliams, Beulah Knox, Ouida d'Abreu and Mary Heaf.

B.A. Degree *(1951)*. Cecil Isola, Ian Bailey and Jimmie Milliken.

Adelaide Hospital *(1953)*.

Graduation Day. Three new Doctors. Dr. Beulah Knox, Dr. Mary Heaf and Dr. Margaret McMullan.

M.B. Graduation Day with May Ringrose *(1953)*.

B.A. Degree. Face view *(1951)*.

The First M.B.

On my return, those of us who had passed the pre-med proceeded to the first year of medicine. All my friends had succeeded, and for the next 18 months, the subjects to be studied in depth were bio-chemistry, physiology and anatomy. Anatomy was particularly difficult, as I did not enjoy ever, a lifeless body staring at me. I would now have to endure for the next 18 months: the smell of strong formalin; two rows of bodies, 12 in all; covered by white sheets and on movable trolleys. I had never seen a dead body. Around the large ventilated and well-lit Anatomy room, lay plenty of body parts, all beautifully dissected by previous anatomists, encased in glass, and preserved in formalin. They covered the walls. A large wooden chest with more body parts was available, on request, for all who wished to study a particular section. It was weird, but essential, to the understanding of the body. I began to have doubts as to whether I would continue, and for the next two months had sleeping difficulties and nightmares. With Professor Erskine at the helm and especially lecturer Dr Blanche Weekes, that hurdle was overcome. In order to ensure that the subject was taken seriously, we were kept continuously at the high level alert, with fortnightly spot Anatomy tests, and end of term examinations. By the time the course ended 18 months later, Grays Anatomy was well encased into my cerebrum.

Professor Fearon was our bio-chemistry lecturer and always interesting. With Professor Torrens in the field of physiology, the two laid down my foundations for the body's normal functions. Both were exceptional lecturers. In the case of Torrens, we had a good, kind and easily accessible professor. He epitomised the good Irish doctor abroad, and had all the qualifications to become the Dean of the Medical School. He succeeded Professor Bigger. Anatomy was the most difficult subject of all. It required considerable brain power; long hours of theoretical and practical work; no short-cuts and an abundance of 'grin and bear it'. Once passed, you were half-way home, to your eventual qualification. After the examinations of April 1950, we now embarked into the pathology of the body, its bacteriology, pharmacology and medical jurisprudence. Again we were blessed by the high standard of teaching, from doctors of the calibre, of Professors Stewart and Bigger; Doctors Wallace and Micks and many others.

Commons, Weyhausen and Carmel

In the Dining Hall, reserved at that time for males, the Undergraduate's gown had to be worn. Dinner in College was a grand formal occasion, and you had to look clean and smart, wearing an appropriate tie. Only resident students partook in its nightly feast; at least that is what it was for those who had been in wartime Britain. The food was excellent, five star and well served. Prayers prior to dining were mandatory. Beer was provided free by Guinness. On Friday, fish was compulsory for all. All resident males of the College attended.

At 9 p.m., all Junior and Senior Freshmen (and the gated ones) had to attend night-roll! At exactly 9 o'clock the Front Gates closed, and there was no way you could leave the University after that time (P 15) This kept junior students from perceived temptations. There were none visible in the Dublin streets and no night clubs to excite one, and lead to a premature bankruptcy.

Women were barred from living in College, and any seen after 6 p.m. were quickly 'apprehended' (P 13, P14). To entertain a young lady in your room, during office hours, required permission. A reason had to be given and a coffee hardly an appropriate excuse, since due notice of your intention had to be given days before. Trinity was surrounded by an abundance of coffee shops. A lunch date in your flat would have been a valid excuse, but none of the students I knew could have fried a sausage, and the Warden and Junior Dean knew this. However during Trinity Week, parties were held, throughout the College, and ladies were allowed to remain till nine: exactly. Not all was work. There were islands of enjoyment, parties, evening balls, and of course, love.

Carmel

At the Country Shop in St Stephen's Green, I met a young medical student, from University College, by name Carmel Casserly (P 17 my left). In simple terms she bowled me over. Unfortunately, I met her three months before Easter, and now with our vacation on, I would not be seeing her again until the summer term. This was not good enough, and with my Joburg friend, Ernest Weyhausen, we planned part of our Easter holidays to co-incide with a call at her home in Nenagh, Co. Tipperary. Male determination and love can go a long way. We decided to cycle to her home, via the longest possible route, in order to ensure no parental suspicions: from Dublin to Cork; to Tralee; to Listowel; to Limerick and ending in Nenagh. We slept in hotels and barns later on, as we were short of cash. Barns on bitterly cold nights with my allergies to hay led to a few uncomfortable nights. Upon arrival at Nenagh, Ernest acted as my decoy, and engaged Carmel's family as if he were her boyfriend. The era of love and romance was still alive. Irish fathers were highly suspicious of men's intentions and foreign men even more so. We spent two glorious days with them and left for Dublin on our bicycles, our mission having been accomplished. But 25 miles down the road with sore bottoms, and 80 miles more to go, we hitched two lifts in lorries: one to Maryborough (Port Laoise) and the other to Dublin, our final destination. Our love continued for a further five months and then as so often happens to the young, fizzled out.

Clean Fun

Ernest was always ready to enjoy life to the very full and on more than one occasion I joined in the fun. Post-commencement or Graduation day was invariably a noisy occasion, for those lucky enough to graduate. At one, the Graduates handcuffed themselves, presumably by borrowing the handcuffs from the adjoining Pearse Street police station. Rudderless and with no-where to go, Ernest led them to the conga tune, out of the College, and onto the College Green. There he clamped the leader to the immovable iron bench, in front of the Grattan Statue. 'Cecil' shouted Ernest, 'clamp him to the College railings'. This I did, as I was holding the last man's handcuff. This human chain now obstructed Dublin's most congested thoroughfare. We both walked back into Trinity. We had created a major traffic jam, which would only be relieved by whoever had the keys: the police. For two months, we kept well away from the Front Gate, but the traffic policemen knew who we were. For my remaining years at Trinity, whenever I crossed the police point at Lower Grafton Street, the policeman would stop the traffic; acknowledge me with a smile, and salute. The era of clean fun was still in vogue.

In another spontaneous incident, following our pre-lunch lecture, the University's Fabian Society was in noisy mode; demonstrating and parading though the College grounds. It sought new members. A few of us including Ernest, decided a bucket of water, from my window would cool them down, since they were heading our way. One or two others joined us and they preferred the fire hydrant, but before it could be put to full use, I saw the Junior Dean, 'the law enforcer', leave his Rubric rooms (P 3). It was lunch hour and most of the lectures had finished. The Fabian demonstration had created a student pandemonium. It attracted Trinity's three most beautiful girls: Iris Quinn, Joan Shellenberg and a friend, to my floor. Due to the crowds outside, the Dean's passage was partially obstructed, so all the males, were able to leave unnoticed before his arrival, but not the 'belles'. I showed them to my bedroom. "Quickly hide under the bed. The bed cover will conceal you". As the Dean knocked on my door, I acted as if I was fully engrossed in my work but I was a poor actor. He asked "May I see your kitchen?" "Yes Sir."

As he found nothing, he asked to be taken to my bedroom and coal-room, which lay across the communal landing. As I opened the bedroom door, from under the bed, a lady's shoe attached to a shapely quarter of a leg could be clearly deciphered, not only by me but the Dean as well.

"Madam will you please identify yourself, by coming out from under the bed". Out came the first girl, but as the quarter leg still remained another polite exhortation. A second girl came out, with the quarter leg still in situ. He now knew there were three under my bed. "Report to your warden today", he told them. And turning towards me, "Mr Isola report to my rooms at 9.30 p.m." As he was about to leave my landing, he turned round, and in a low voice said, "Greedy." I was terrified for the next nine hours, for the punishment was still awaiting me. I was fined 10 shillings. "Can you afford this amount?" "Yes Sir." "Good. You will report for night-roll till the end of the present academic term." (P 15)

Night-roll consisted of attending physically outside the Dining Hall, when the Junior Dean would call out your name, and visually confirm before recording it. It meant you could not leave College after 9 p.m. and you would have been a fool to have done so. For the next two months, I was socially dead, which was not as bad as one might think. It encouraged a little extra work in my pleasant confines. I missed three or four dinner dances and several parties, which I could socially well afford.

The Liffey Stuff ("Guinness")

In Spain I used to offer a cigarette or packet of cigarettes to the frontier's Guardia Civil to ensure ease of passage. The same but with a different flavour, I applied to the Front Gate's porters. Whether it was at the legally permitted time of arrival (before 11 p.m.) or not, a couple of bottles of the "Liffey Stuff" always did the trick. I was never reported for being late. Unlike other students, who preferred to risk scaling the railings or rough the night, I preferred the gentlemen's way of entry, albeit for a small price. It worked well.

Bookmakers and Fiat 500

Trinity was surrounded by bookmakers' shops and I often spoke to Dennis Packham (P 22), a fellow student and friend of the racing animal. He always had good information. Rarely a week passed without a flutter. On one occasion, I mistook the exceptionally good horse 'Arctic Gold', for the not so good 'Arctic Silver', in my 5 shilling treble. That mistake enriched me by an amount big enough to buy a second-hand Fiat 500. Unfortunately, from day one, it was a disastrous buy. After refusing all forms of mechanical exhortations, Ernest Weyhausen suggested we should bring the engine to my bedroom and work on it. So we did. He identified and corrected the fault. My knowledge of the engine was very much restricted, but Ernest appeared to be a born genius. We carried the engine from my bedroom to Botany Bay, and installed it back on the mule. It started at first go. We went for a drive. The engine worked to perfection. That evening, I met my second Irish love, Jean Robertson (P 21). I wanted to impress her with my second hand automobile. With Jean onboard, the car was once again emotional in its behaviour, for after several unplanned stops, it eventually refused to budge. I accompanied her back to Garville Road: on foot. Returning back to my stubborn mule, I kick-started her once again. It was now dark. The lights had to be switched on. Ernest had inadvertently connected the light wires to the horn, and the horn wires to the lights. So long as I kept my hand pressed hard on the horn, the car lights stayed on. As the horn was imbedded in the centre of the driving wheel, I could not keep my fingers there, when cornering. At one of those corners a police car saw me and turned to follow me. I escaped by driving in an area where there was enough room for a small Fiat 500 but not for a police car. I lost him but not for long, for 10 days later, I received a summons to appear in court. I was petrified. Fortunately the friendly judge who had difficulty in keeping his face straight, understood my plight and dismissed the case. The car was sold back to the garage for half the price and this information helped the judge in coming to a good verdict.

Ernest, like myself, was a student visitor to Ireland. He came from Johannesburg, South Africa, and after a long love forage, married his one real love: Varna. I was their best man in Exeter, England. He was brilliant with his hands, highly intelligent and could adapt to any unexpected circumstances which arose. He would have reached the zenith of our profession, had his premature and unexpected death not occurred in Bulawayo, Zimbabwe.

My other good friend Michael Drummond (P 21), whom I first met in 1947, introduced me to most of the cinema managers and as a result I rarely queued and often gained free admission. At one event, the manager of the Adelphi Cinema required my urgent help. At the first Irish Film Festival, two hours before the show was to start, he'd received a last minute V.I.P cancellation. So he asked could I come to the cinema immediately; physically fill the vacant seat and be in dinner jacket. I did. I sat in the front row of the dress circle, a few seats from the President of Ireland, Sean T. O'Kelly. After the show, I shook hands with him and met the actors Richard Todd, Anne Todd and Christine Norden. I sat with Mícheál MacLiamor, Ireland's most famous and colourful character actor and discussed the theatre over coffee. Another of Michael Drummond's introductions was to an air-hostess, in an era when supreme looks and manners mattered to Aer Lingus. On two occasions I was invited to their annual dance: first at Colliston

Airport (Dublin) and the second at the Gresham Hotel. On the second occasion, we had the captain of the English Rugby team, who also played for Cambridge University, in our table of six.

Rugby

I played Rugby for Trinity's third fifteen; a short time for Monkston's first where we played against the N.I.F.C. at Stormont and for Sir Patrick Dun's (P 21, P22) in the Hospitals' Cup. In one of the matches at Lansdowne Road, I badly collided with a St Vincent's player, and was carried off. Several days in hospital, taunted by the student nurses, ended my not too illustrious Rugby career. Headaches following exercises was the cause. Squash was also a victim. But being a member of the University Rugby Club gave me the opportunity to be a steward at all the international matches at Lansdowne Road, and best of all, for free. I watched Ireland win the Triple Crown for three years running. It was at a time when the Universities of all-Ireland played an important part in the formation of the Irish teams. Robin Roe and Gerry Murphy were two of the Irish Rugby Team that I knew as a result of my playing for Trinity's third; Karl Mullen was another from National. Karl and I were both medical students but in different hospitals.

Living in the centre of Dublin and in its most peaceful area, was the opportunity that hundreds of my fellow students inadvertently missed. All the opportunities that came my way were attended to. I saw, and was present on O'Connell Bridge at the midnight firing of guns, on Ireland's accession, as a nation, in 1948. I watched all the St Patrick's Day's parades; An Tostal, and listened to a brilliant speaker and young politician, Séan McBride, outside the College.

He later acquired fame in the field of human rights. If there was anything to be seen or heard, I was there, thanks to my city centre residency.

During my first M.B. year, a few of us tried to form a Catholic Association, within the University. We had the support of some of the Catholic lecturers. I was trying to organise a similar grouping as existed at Oxford, where my brother Willie, was President of the Newman Society. There the Jesuits from Campion Hall partook such as Fr. D'Arcy. S.J. and others. Alas, the Catholic Bishop of Dublin would not see us, and by my third year in medicine, I realised the impossibility of any headway in the years ahead (P 9, P11). I was seeking a Jesuit as our advisor. Whilst the subject of religion, occasionally raised its head at Commons (dinner), I had no problem in any discussion. At my 50th Medical Graduation Anniversary, I attended mass in Trinity's chapel: a welcome sign. This could have been achieved years earlier, had the forces of confrontation been replaced by those favouring co-operation and Christian values.

The Dublin Hospitals—The Second M.B.

Following my Second M.B. I was now half-way to the finals. Medicine, surgery, obstetrics, gynaecology and psychiatry were next in line. My class was now to split into several student branches, depending on which hospital you went to. Dublin hospitals were numerous and small in size. Those that were open to Trinity's students were Sir Patrick Dun's, the Adelaide, the Royal City of Dublin, Dr Stevens and the Meath hospital. I selected Sir Patrick Dun's. It was here that I attended most of my ward rounds, clinics and had a three-month residency. The hospital was small by U.K.

standards, but the quality of its teachers was well above the norm. There was Freddie Gill, Robert Woods, Seymour Heatley, Tom O'Neill, and George Fegan on the surgical side. Professor Micks, Jackie Wallace, Heber McMahon, and Joe Kirker served the medical side. Freddie Gill, the senior surgeon, put the fear of God into one, if one did not answer correctly or well. It was said that the basis for the Sir Lancelot character in the 'Carry On' series 'Doctor in the House', was based on him. It certainly rang a familiar note when I saw the films. The lecturers that caught my interest most were the doctors to whom I could talk on a man-to-man basis and without doubt were George Fegan (later Professor of Surgery) and Joe Kirker. All were excellent. As long as the monthly hospital card was signed, you could attend your hospital of choice. Professor Synge, Professor Henry, Mr Stokes, Doctors Parsons and Brendan O'Brien were my selected non-Sir Patrick Dun's consultants and all gave information unlikely to be forgotten. In the case of Dr Parsons, after testing a diabetic's urine with Fehling's solution, he enquired of his entourage of ten medical students, whether one of us would taste the urine. Though we had all tasted our own, and made comments on it, it was quite another thing to taste someone else. "In my young days," went the elderly Dr Parsons "that is how we diagnosed diabetes, by tasting the urine. Those that tasted sweet were diabetics." There were no volunteers.

There was a very strict no-nonsense attitude to cleanliness and all students had to be properly dressed, shaved, hair groomed, clean clothes and all that goes with a doctor's presence. One erring medical student arrived at a ward-round, unshaven and tie-less. He was suspended from hospital work for seven days and lectured in front of our group. He learnt his lesson.

Ethics was an important part of our teaching, and the causes of negligence drummed into our young minds. "Examine every patient and listen to what they say. If you do not, the patient might have a good case against you for negligence. A misdiagnosis is easier to defend legally, if the patient has been examined". If your idea of coming to Trinity's medical school was to relax, you quickly were made aware that this school was not for the idle. At every lecture, the number of those not attending was recorded. Following the ward-round, the consultant's initial was required on a special date card, which was replaced and checked at the medical school, monthly. Tests were regularly carried out and marks were exhibited outside the medical school's office. A few could not keep up and left, but the majority slogged their way through, with long hours of hard work.

The Specialised Hospitals

I was always keen to get on with my work, as most others were, yet on one occasion, I overdid it. Having returned from my annual summer holiday in Gibraltar, our class had to attend the practical side of obstetrics, at the Rotunda Hospital. The first baby delivery was carried out effortlessly by the sister-in-charge of the theatre. It looked so easy, that any old fool could do it. Now one student was asked to volunteer. Refreshed by my summer vacation, up went my foolish hand. It was a solo one. Red faced and hearing sniggers behind my back, I walked to the semi-anaesthetised patient, in a trembling state of nerves. With the full cooperation of the sister, I 'delivered' the patient. As I carried the slimey baby, it slipped between my hands, but luckily my Rugby training, prevented a disaster.

New-born babies are like Rugby balls on a muddy field: slippery, heavy, and in this case, with a well coated layer of grease.

The Rotunda with its district service could not have been bettered. For the first time I was now called a doctor. As part of our Rotunda training, four of us working as a group would attend to all normal deliveries in the deprived areas of North Dublin. The Rotunda's ante-natal care ensured that only normal deliveries would take place in the district. Most of the patients we attended were the poor of the poorest. When one of us, considered that we had a problem on our hands, a call to base was IMMEDIATELY responded to, by a senior doctor. A duty roster existed and each group knew the likelihood of when he was to be called. Within minutes of your room bell ringing, you had to report at the gate. No excuses were tolerated for lateness. This was an emergency.

At Grange Gorman, the mental hospital, matters were different and though improvements in psychiatry were still not in the pipeline, it was not pleasant to see the suffering within. At the Royal Victoria Eye Hospital the excellent eye specialists gave you their time and the one I remembered most was the great Somerville-Large.

Rathgar

After leaving my rooms in Trinity, I spent two years in digs, and the difference between living in College and my new found accommodation was enormous. The University was far better. As I lived in Rathgar, I bought a small cycle engine for my bicycle. This gave me better propulsion. Unfortunately the engine was too powerful for my brakes, and obviously this had not been taken into account by the makers. On my way to Rathgar without night lights,

I was stopped by a policeman. Unfortunately, I was in fast mode and one of the rubber brakes departed and hit the policeman on his face. The cycle stopped 40 yards further on. I was summoned to court, defended myself and received a warning. The end-result was a Vespa Scooter, which would now revolutionise my university life, for unknown to me, I was only months away from meeting, May, my future wife.

I knew Dublin at a time when it had little in wealth, but was rich in standards. Crime was virtually nil and you could walk the streets at all hours of the day, night and in smog without fear whatever. There were no 'druggies' either in the streets or in hospital. The trams, as a means of transport within the city area, existed for most of my time there. I enjoyed the final ride from Nelsons Pillar to Kingston, now renamed Dun Laoghaire. I walked back. I had a bird's eye view of Dublin from the top of Nelsons Pillar, later reduced to rubble by the I.R.A. I learnt much about Ireland, its people and of course its troubled history. I was able to understand all sides of the English-created Irish problem since I had read widely and listened to many, whose knowledge was well above normal.

Jimmie Milliken, Ian Bailey and Others

I met Jimmie Milliken in my pre-med year and our friendship, lasted throughout our lives (P7, P17, P24, P28). He fell in love, early in his career, with a beautiful redhead, full of laughter and personality, named Brenda McMechan. She lived in Belfast. His love for Brenda allowed me to visit the north of Ireland, since I accompanied him there on many occasions. His good friend Marshall Jones owned a chain of china shops, both in the north and south. Jimmie and I were invited to his annual staff parties where we stayed as guests of the company, at well known northern hotels. As a result I saw Portrush, the Giant's Causeway, Ballymena, Belfast and many other places of Ulster interest. On our return, we always chose to go the longest way back to Dublin, since that route passed Brenda's home and that was always paramount in his mind. The excuse was good. On one occasion, my invitation to Hollywood Belfast, led me to believe, rather naively, that Belfast's Hollywood was akin to its namesake in the United States. It was worth visiting. We slept on the floor of her house for two days: alright for Jimmie in love, but not for his 'chaperone', who woke up with a sore back. Without Jimmie's magnetic attraction to Brenda, I would most certainly have not seen its beautiful north and understood its people. Jimmie was always my driver, and a good one at that.

Following our graduation, he remained in Dublin, but when an opportunity arose, temporarily migrated to Houston, U.S.A., where he worked under de Bakey, the world's most renowned vascular surgeon. Back in Dublin he followed the new breakthrough varicose vein treatment introduced by Professor George Fegan with the help of a Cambridge researcher, Oliver Murphy, who later graduated in medicine at T.C.D. Jimmie became one of Dublin's most famous vascular surgeons and an eminence in the treatment of varicose veins. In the early 60's, Jimmie operated on my veins and tied my interconnecting ones. "Cecil, I have left your veins intact. Should you get a heart attack, come back, and I will replace your diseased coronary vessels. Your veins are ready for transplanting". The era of coronary by-passes was about to cross the Atlantic. I was now ready should the occasion arise. Fortunately, to date, it has not. Jimmie is now retired.

Jimmie and George wanted me to introduce the new varicose vein treatment in Gibraltar and I was prepared to start it. But with no grey hairs, local political aversion to medical progress and the substantial costs involved, I desisted. It was a pity for many Gibraltarians would have benefited from such treatment. At the time of writing, it is the one now used worldwide.

Ian Bailey, (P 24, P25, P28) was another of our student group and a very hard worker, as indeed we all were. But unlike Jimmie and me, he was registered at the Adelaide Hospital, and became scarce at social events. The old adage, "that behind every great man lies a good woman" could not have been truer. Like Jimmie and I, he was stunned by Ruth, a co-worker at the Adelaide. She became his wife. He pursued neurosurgery and must have been involved in dealing with many of the casualties, during Northern Ireland's troubles.

While all our lectures took place in the medical school, subjects of special interest were held in the hospital. Trinity's hospitals were all small and all blessed with an abundance of good teachers and consultants. "Common things occur commonly" and the consultants and teachers sought to impress that fact upon our young minds. With time that view paid handsomely, for I could compare my work with others, who had a deeper knowledge of the diseases that rarely came up, and missed out on the commoner ones.

Non-Medical Friends

My friends were not only from the medical school but from other faculties as well. Evan Anagnostros (P17, P18, P19, P21) a colonial

Kenyan, who boxed for our University; David Lindsay, an engineering student from England; Da Souza from Portugal and many others. There were also other medical students, who were a few years behind me at Trinity like Moira Fann (P21), and Bill Tweddell (P19) at the Royal College of Surgeons. Men like Felim Meade, Furzi Hogan and a host of others formed our social groups.

May: My Future Wife

It was in April 1952, that my bachelor life and university pranks would come to an end, for my life was about to change forever. A few of us had decided to go dancing to Mount Pleasant Tennis Club, as it was Saturday and a rainless evening. Whilst dancing, I saw two beautiful faces though the club's window and one dazzled me. I had been struck by lightning. A quick exit to the club's grounds received the usual response of the women of the day. I came back to the club house empty handed. I however kept my eyes wide open, just in case they changed their minds and entered the club's premises. She eventually came in, in a group of five: three men and two women. All I now had to do was to ensure that this young lady should dance with me. I knew the secretary and band-leader well. "The next dance is an 'excuse me', and when the music stops, ladies must dance with the man on their right". I was guaranteed this partner for much of the evening. In effect, my good friend the band-leader guaranteed my near monopoly of her. From now on my life changed, as any student knows, when stunned. Her name was May Ringrose (S4-7) and she came from Limerick; her friend Mary O'Brien was from Co. Mayo. Lunch in Trinity's Dining Hall would now become a rarity as women were barred from eating there (P13). If I were to share my lunch hour, I would have to eat elsewhere, and I did!

Whereas before I had five evenings for study, now there would be less. Fortunately May had to be in her digs, at 36 Leeson Park, by 11 p.m. The night was still young for further studies. To have a girlfriend in your final year of academia can be difficult, but the subjects were far easier to absorb than the anatomy of my earlier years.

With a Vespa scooter, about to make its mark on the nascent Dublin market and one already in my possession, I was well-placed to see the surrounding countryside, with my new found love. Within a very short period, I met her sister, Rita: another beautiful and intelligent girl; and within months, her two younger sisters, Alice and Nell, in the later stage of adolescence. The beauty gene was strong in this genome (S 5).

Hospital clinics, university lectures, social events, and a life equal to post-war Gibraltar, the Dublin scene I knew in 1953, would never be bettered. Bill Tweddell, David Lindsay, Evan Anagastorous, Paris Panayottou (P 19) and many others were now moving into their graduation and subsequent exits from Dublin. Some of them had cars (and one a plane) and on public holidays, we visited many of the areas with un-paralleled beauty surrounding Dublin.

Chapter 8

IN ABSENTIA. 1945-56.

In Gibraltar all was 'Quiet on the Isola Front, and no Isola stood for the 1945 City Council elections (N). The era of the political parties had arrived with the A.A.C.R.: the Advanced Association for Civil Rights. Its main aim was geared at the military's abuse of power within the Garrison. It had the opposite effect. It divided the community into two camps: the Colonials (right of centre) and the Colonised (left of centre): the party versus the non-party independents and the introduction of the colonial concept of 'Divide and Rule', which up till then did not exist.

By 1944, the first evacuees began to return home: many from London and Ballymena (Northern Ireland). They had been evacuated by the military for their own safety. The Beccles' article of 1945 recorded part of the problem (N). I was not here. Beccles was.

I was also away for the First Legislative Council elections, which were held in 1951. In that election, my late father was the only member to be elected on the first count (O 1). H.R.H. Prince Philip

(O) was here to open our First Legislative Council. Fortunately from my point of view, cameras were returning to the post-war market, even though to many of its users, they were too complicated for personal and general use. Nonetheless, there were a few who purchased them and used them.

Three years later, in 1954, H.M. Queen Elizabeth II (R) paid her first and only official visit to Gibraltar, to the great annoyance of General Franco, the self-proclaimed 'Caudillo of Peace'. The camera once again recorded some of the events, of that period.

IN ABSENTIA
THE FIRST LEGISLATIVE COUNCIL.

THE ELECTION RESULTS

Albert R. Isola was the first and only elected member to the legislature on the first count, with 2002 preferences votes. Panayotti was second with 1058, and was subsquently elected on the second vote.

	First Count Vote
Bianchi	106
Bruzón	671
Hassan	1009
Huart	434
Isola	2022
Panayotti	1058
Patrón	567
Risso	1112
Serfaty	71

Biañchi	106 más	9	115
Bruzón	671 más	88	759
Hassan	1009 más	91	1100
Huart	434 más	25	459
Panayotti	1058 más	198	1256
Patrón	567 más	399	966
Risso	1112 más	28	1140
Serfaty	71 más	8	79

Second count vote. Panayotti elected.

IN ABSENTIA.

O.

Inauguration of the First Legislative Council.

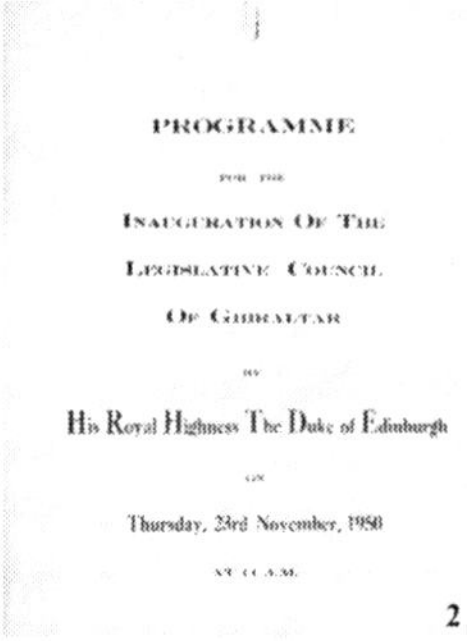

PROGRAMME
FOR THE
INAUGURATION OF THE
LEGISLATIVE COUNCIL
OF GIBRALTAR
BY
His Royal Highness The Duke of Edinburgh
ON
Thursday, 23rd November, 1950
AT 11 A.M.

Members of Legislative Council

President
 The Governor
 His Excellency General Sir Kenneth A. N. Anderson, K.C.B., M.C.

Ex Officio Members
1. The Colonial Secretary
 The Honourable B. J. O'Brien, C.M.G.
2. The Attorney-General
 The Honourable G. C. Ross, K.C.
3. The Financial Secretary
 The Honourable A. E. Cook, J.P.

Elected Members
4. The Honourable A. R. Isola, J.P.
5. The Honourable P. Russo, Jr.
6. The Honourable A. J. Risso
7. The Honourable J. A. Hassan, J.P.
8. The Honourable Major J. Patron, O.B.E., M.C., J.P.

Nominated Members
9. The Honourable H. J. Coelho
10. The Honourable J. Hayward, O.B.E.

Clerk of Council
 E. H. Davis, Esq.

H.R.H. The Duke of Edinburgh on his way to open the First Legislative Council in 1951.

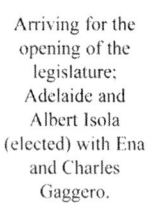

Arriving for the opening of the legislature; Adelaide and Albert Isola (elected) with Ena and Charles Gaggero.

IN ABSENTIA.   O.

The Legislature with H.R.H. The Duke of Edimburgh, and the President and Governor Sir Kenneth Anderson K.C.B., M.C. *Albert Isola (sitting 1st left).*

An invitation to H.M.Y. Britannia.

A Menu.

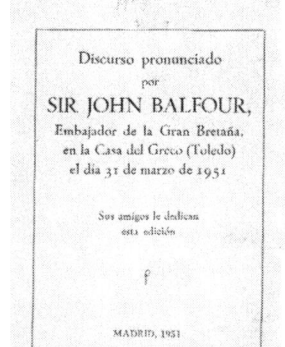

Meeting Sir John Balfour, British Ambassador to Madrid, 1951. Within 4 months of being elected!

The only British decoration my father accepted: The Coronation Medal. "You cannot serve 2 masters: the people and the Colonial Government".

IN ABSENTIA.

O.

The Moroccan Peace Medal. Signed Primo Rivera. Awarded 16th January 1930.

Albert Isola entering the House of Assembly.

OBITUARY.
GIBRALTAR CHRONICLE.

Death of Mr. A. R. Isola

HE WAS A FEARLESS ADVOCATE OF CAUSES IN WHICH HE BELIEVED

THE death occurred at home in his sleep in the early hours of yesterday morning, of Mr. Albert R. Isola, Q.C., J.P., leader of the local Bar and, until recently when his health declined, one of Gibraltar's leading political and public figures. He was 61.

Mr. Isola was present at the Society for Musical Culture's concert on Monday evening, and stayed on at the Rock Hotel until quite late, chatting to His Lordship the Roman Catholic Bishop and other friends.

A brilliant advocate and past-master in the art of cross-examination, Mr. Isola was educated at the Christian Brothers' School in Line Wall Road and at Stonyhurst.

He was called to the local Bar in 1920, made a Justice of the Peace in 1931 and King's Counsel in 1951. His last appearance in Court was at the ceremonial opening of the Legal Year on October 3 last.

Mr. Isola served on Executive Council in pre-war days and became the first Gibraltarian to be elected to Legislative Council, topping the poll on the first count at the 1950 election.

He was elected again in 1953 but in the 1956 elections, although he stood, he advised his followers to give their first preference to his son, the Hon. P. J. Isola.

Throughout his 30 years of public service, Don Alberto served on innumerable Boards and Committees. A keen race-goer, he was President of the Gibraltar Jockey Club and a life-President of the Mediterranean Racing Club. He was also President of the Casino Calpe.

Equally brilliant with pen

A fearless advocate of the causes in which he believed, Mr. Isola was, in his hey-day, as brilliant with his pen as he was with his speeches.

There will be many who remember the sting in his articles signed 'Beccles' in "El Anunciador" in pre-war days.

Of his forensic ability it used to be said: If your case is weak in law, consult Mr. Isola. If it is strong go to his great rival in the legal and political sphere, the late Mr. S. P. Triay.

Mr. Isola is mourned by his mother, widow, three sons, a daughter and a brother. His two elder sons are barristers, like himself, while the youngest is a doctor. His daughter, on holiday in England when her father died, is married to Mr. E. M. Russo.

Mr. & Mrs. Russo expect to fly back for the funeral, which is at present timed to take place at 10.45 a.m. this morning, from 3, Secretary's Lane, with Mass 'Corpore Praesente' at the Cathedral of St. Mary the Crowned at 11 a.m.

Gibraltar Chronicle, 26th October 1960.

"Our loss is great"

FUNERAL OF MR. A. R. ISOLA

THE Cathedral of St. Mary the Crowned was packed to capacity yesterday at 11 a.m. for the Mass "Corpore Praesente" for the late Mr. Albert R. Isola, at which His Lordship the Rt. Rev. John F. Healy, Roman Catholic Bishop, officiated prior to the burial at the family vault at North Front cemetery.

The funeral procession left deceased's residence in Secretary's Lane 15 minutes earlier, the chief mourners being his three sons and brother. Mrs. E. M. Russo, his daughter, was at the Cathedral with her husband, having arrived by air from London on Tuesday evening.

His Excellency the Governor, General Sir Charles Keightley, was represented by his Aide-de-Camp, Captain J. J. F. Scott, The Royal Dragoons.

Others who attended included the Hon. Mr. Justice Flaxman, His Worship the Mayor, The Hon. Colonial Secretary, The Speaker of the Legislative Council, Members of the Executive, Legislative and City Councils, judiciary, Consular Corps, legal profession, police and representatives from commercial firms, public bodies, Unions, institutions and clubs, as well as many acquaintances and friends.

There were over 60 wreaths and other floral tributes.

Earlier, in the Court of First Instance, a tribute was paid by Acting Judge J. E. Alcantara, who said: "I think of him as a friend who was always willing to help and advise the junior members of the Bar.

"As one of Her Majesty's Counsel and leader of the Gibraltar Bar, he commanded the respect which is due to a barrister of integrity, of a high degree of skill, and of unlimited industry on his clients' behalf. His sudden passing is indeed a lamentable affair. Our loss is great."

Mr. A. V. Stagnetto associated himself with the Judge's remarks on behalf of the Bar, the case before the Court being adjourned.

Gibraltar Chronicle, 28th October 1960.

OBITUARY.

THE STONYHURST MAGAZINE.

ALBERT RICHARD ISOLA, Q.C., J.P.
(1914—1918)

The death of Albert Isola occurred very suddenly, at the age of sixty-one, on 25th October. We offer our sympathy to his widow and sons, William (1935), Cecil (1938) and Peter (1938), to his daughter, Mrs E. M. Russo, and to all the family in their sad loss.

Albert Isola was at Stonyhurst for four years, arriving from Gibraltar when he was fifteen in September 1914 (ten years before his younger brother, Ernest), going straight into Poetry and then spending three years in Rhetoric. In his last year he was Head of the Line, as were his uncle, Horace Parodi before him (in 1886-87), and his nephew, Charles Isola after him (in 1958-59). He was also prefect of the Sodality and captain of the Football XI. Turning over the pages of the back numbers of *The Stonyhurst Magazine* one frequently comes across his name—in plays, in the records of the S.U.D.S. and in the higher ranks of the O.T.C. Before he left Stonyhurst he had started reading law and in 1920 he passed his finals and was called to the Gibraltar Bar. In 1931 he was made a Justice of the Peace and in 1951 King's Counsel; at the time of his death he was leader of the Gibraltar Bar. As a lawyer he was very successful. He had a clear, logical mind, was an excellent speaker and won many well-deserved triumphs. The *Gibraltar Chronicle* described him as 'a brilliant advocate and past-master in the art of cross-examination' and in court on the day of his funeral the Judge said 'he commanded the respect which is due to a barrister of integrity, of a high degree of skill and of unlimited industry on his clients' behalf'. He was equally respected as a Justice of the Peace.

On 1st November 1943 it was announced that 'His Majesty has been pleased to approve the appointment of Albert Richard Isola, Esquire, J.P., as unofficial member of the Executive Council of Gibraltar for a period of three years'. When the Legislative Council was set up under the Constitution of 1950 he decided at the last minute to stand and topped the poll —'the first Gibraltarian', says the *Gibraltar Chronicle*, 'to be elected'. (He was elected again in 1953, and in 1956, his son, Peter, was elected, filling the place vacated by his father.) A month later he was again appointed a member of the Executive Council. His services to Gibraltar, before, during and after the war, were valuable; he was on innumerable Boards and Committees, yet he always remained very much of an independent in politics with the interests of Gibraltar and the people in his mind. He was quite prepared to stand alone, a fearless advocate of causes in which he believed. In consequence of his legal and political work he was one of Gibraltar's leading political and public figures; he was also president of the Gibraltar Jockey Club and a life president of the Mediterranean Racing Club.

He was married in January 1924 in Gibraltar Cathedral to Miss Adelaide Murto, daughter of Mr and Mrs Matias Murto of Gibraltar.

In recent years his health began to fail, yet he made a good recovery from illness more than once and continued his work, says the local newspaper *El Calpense*, with even greater vigour as he was determined not to be overcome by ill health, but when death came it came suddenly. The evening before he died he was at a concert and stayed on afterwards talking to the Bishop of Gibraltar and other friends. Requiem Mass was offered at the Cathedral of St Mary the Crowned; His Lordship the Bishop officiated. Apart from the family, the large congregation included the representative of the Governor, and the Chief Justice, the Mayor, the Colonial Secretary, the Speaker of the Legislative Council and representatives of the Councils, the Judiciary, and Consular Corps, and many other public bodies and business firms as well as friends and acquaintances.

We may assure his family and relations of our prayers for the respose of his soul. May he rest in peace.

Chapter 9

HOSPITALS AND MARRIAGE

With my degrees in hand by 1953, and pre-registration appointments to follow, I bade farewell to May, my friends and Dublin. Bill Tweddell, a Stonyhurst friend a few years behind me at the Royal College of Surgeons had suggested I work where his father practised and lived. Dr Bill Tweddell (Snr) was a famous doctor and golfer. In the 30's, he led the British Ryder Cup Team to victory. His father suggested that I apply to the Dudley Guest Hospital, for it was an excellent hospital for hard work and experience. I got accepted, following my written application for the post of house surgeon to the orthopaedic, E.N.T. and surgical consultants. I was also to be casualty officer for after 'office' hours: four appointments for the salary of one. My salary was £250 per annum without tax or the costs of emoluments. The emoluments consisted of a comfortable room and full pension and like the tax came out of my basic salary. Cash in hand was £3 per week. For that salary, I was to be on duty for 24 hours a day for 3 weeks; with a half day off on Wednesday;

1 hour for Sunday's Holy Mass; one free weekend every three, commencing at 2pm on Friday and ending Monday at 9am. Duty meant duty and you would have been dismissed from your post if you had been found wanting. The pre-registration year was the important one, for without it you could not register with the G.M.C. (General Medical Council), and therefore be fit to practise.

Within days of my arrival at the Dudley Guest Hospital, I was thrown into the very deep end of surgical practice: a woman had attempted suicide by slitting her throat to the larynx. My request for outside help fell on deaf ears. "Are you not a doctor?" "Have you not stitched before?" "Was anatomy not in your course?" As all my answers were in the affirmative, the consultant replied "Well, do it". With the help of Alex Meldrum, the young anaesthetist, an anatomy book and a trembling hand, my first surgical assignment ended in success. Tragically though, as predicted by the consultant, the woman succeeded in her original intention, a few days later. Casualty was the area for learning and practising. After many failed attempts at fracture reduction, my first perfect alignment was achieved 2 weeks later. Once I had acquired the technique, few required correction by the registrar or consultant. I saw a considerable number. The orthopaedic clinics lasted for more than four hours, and when the clinic ended, other hospital matters had to be attended to, in much the same way as after the surgical and E.N.T. clinics.

In the E.N.T. field, after a few mishaps, I acquired considerable experience. The clinics were huge and with a fast turnover. I was allowed to perform all the minor operations and by the time I left, I had acquired the best E.N.T. technique possible. Ward-rounds with the consultants, operating sessions and other matters left little or no time for reading. My lunch, on operating days, was had by a quick dash to the dining room between operations. By 9pm we were all exhausted, and retired to the mess, to the black and white television and even then, I was constantly called to casualty. The first casualties began arriving at 6am and were followed in a constant stream with many attempted or actual suicides. The coroner was kept fairly busy. My experience in court went upwards, not because I was the cause, but because a fee of 3 guineas was paid to the attending doctor. Those doctors that had permanent jobs in the area preferred someone else to fill this gap, since it invariably made adverse local news.

On one of my afternoons off, a fatal road accident occurred and the body was brought to the hospital. But the attending doctor did not make a Coroner's report. At 11pm the Coroner's Officer requested my report for 8am the next day. Coroners could be unreasonable, but their requests had to be acceded to without a murmur.

I had never been in an English mortuary and this was to be my first official visit. All alone I walked through the surrounding lawn to the isolated mortuary. There was a full moon. When I unlocked the door and switched the lights on, an array of bodies greeted me. They lay covered in clean white sheets with blue or red crosses on individual trolleys: red was for males. I found my body on the third sheet uplift. Whilst I was recording his injuries, I heard the midnight chimes from the clock above. Within seconds, one of the large refrigerator doors opened with an eerie screech and its lights went on. Inside lay several bodies inline, probably awaiting identification. With a fertile mind, Hollywood films to improve it, and a pair of fast legs, I was out the door and in to the night sister's office in record time. A brandy was prescribed but naturally not in my name. It would have breached hospital rules.

The registrar, who was English, hard working and determined to be a hospital consultant acted as a robot, as indeed we all became. His most memorable words of advice which I tried and failed to impart locally years later were "Cecil, you can admit all patients from G.P.'s who are under 55. Over that age I will take the decision." The era of dumping the old into a hospital bed had begun. It was occurring fairly frequently. There were major difficulties in their rehabilitation. On many occasions, the next of kin bluntly refused to take them home. Full employment for married couples; marriage breakdowns; and the Soviet philosophy of care 'from the cradle to the grave', were the new factors emerging. "Cecil, hospitals are for the sick. We must not allow this hospital to become a residential home for the old". And under his command, we did well.

There were many incidents to fill our hospital lives beyond work, but the one that nearly ended my life was a gunman. He had come at night to casualty with a revolver. He aimed it at me. He demanded that the prettiest hospital nurse be brought to casualty. I had no choice but to call the night sister. "Night sister, this is an order which you must obey. Bring the prettiest nurse to casualty—immediately". Fortunately Dr Alex Meldrum was in the room, and knew me well. He smelt a rat! Within minutes, the sister and the nurse joined me on the bench. Now, all 3 were covered by the gun. Alex not seeing the sister or nurse return called the police. Within a very short time they arrived, disarmed the fugitive and took him away.

Dudley to Dublin by Vespa

Whilst I was entertained by Dr Tweddell and his family on numerous occasions, the social life in Dudley was dead. My bedroom window faced the zoo, and that appeared peaceful. Hospital parties, if they did exist, were not for us, for we were too busy to partake of them. My only social life was still in Dublin. Every third Friday at 2pm, I scootered to Holyhead, for the night crossing to Dun Laoghaire. I returned on the Sunday night ferry, arriving in Holyhead in the early hours of the morning. From there by Vespa to Dudley and ready for work by 9am. There were no excuses accepted had I been late. You had to be there on time, and you were. The roads were empty and eerie. The Welsh early to bed syndrome was visible everywhere. On one occasion, with the ship's damaged propeller, I spent 36 hours in atrocious weather on the Irish Sea, when travelling from Liverpool. But my determination to see my future wife outweighed all the problems that stood in my way. The Guest Hospital was undoubtedly the one that gave me the most confidence and all the necessary expertise, to survive and expand my Gibraltar practice in later years. The costs of entertaining May in Dublin, the Vespa's fuel bill and the ferry costs I paid for from the coroner's inquest fees. My good friend Michael Drummond provided me with free accommodation on those weekends.

Dr Brendan O'Brien—The Meath Hospital

Six months later, completely exhausted, I was accepted to one of Dublin's teaching hospitals: the Meath. I was now under the most eminent physician, Dr Brendan O'Brien. At the Meath the work ethos was different and supervision was intense. There was little I could do, when on casualty duty, for there was always someone above me to whom the case had to be referred. It did not matter whether I was competent or not to deal with the case. Outside my casualty duties, Dr O'Brien guided me through my six month internship superbly well. I learnt much from him. Unlike Dudley's Guest Hospital, there was not enough work to keep me happy. This was fortunate in another respect, for now I had time to further my relationship with May. With doctors covering each other after 5pm and an abundance of them, weekends off and other free periods, I could once again concentrate on the lighter things in life. On the scooter, we explored the scenic areas surrounding Dublin and our love affair flourished.

IN ABSENTIA.
H.M. QUEEN ELIZABETH II VISIT. GIBRALTAR (1954).

R.

H.M.R.Y. Britannia entering Gibraltar.

The Queen's visit. H.M. Queen Elizabeth II with Prince Philip and the Gibraltar Government.

Leaving the King's Chapel. Albert and Adelaide Isola with Rogelia and John Coelho.

Albert R. Isola paying his respects at Victoria Stadium to H.M. Queen Elizabeth II.

Adelaide and Albert Isola entering "The Legislature".

IN ABSENTIA.   R.

Commissioner of Boy Scouts, William Isola escorting H.M. Queen Elizabeth II. Elliot's Steps, Alameda Gardens.

Commissioner of Girl Guides, Patricia Smith with H.M. Queen Elizabeth II, Prince Philip and William Isola. Elliot's Memorial, Alameda Gardens. *(1954)*

Chief Scout: Lord Rowallan.

Chief Scout Lord Rowallan, Commissioner Girl Guides Patricia Smith and Commissioner William Isola taking the Salute at Number 1. Naval Ground.

Lord and Lady Rowallan bid farewell to distinguished guests at R.A.F. Gibraltar Airport.

The Fortress Salutes.

The Fortress Salutes at the Cenotaph on the eleventh hour, the eleventh day of the 11th month.

IN ABSENTIA.

R.

Sir Alfred Patron. Sir Peter Russo. Albert Isola (President). Sir George Gaggero. Sir Edward Cottrell.

Casino Calpe members.

Casino Calpe 1853-1953. Dinner held at Bristol Hotel.

Oxford University Boxing Club. William Isola, front row-1st left. Oxford Blue.

The City Hospital, Edinburgh and the Medical Research Council

As time went on, Dr Brendan O'Brien suggested, and I accepted, that I should work for the Medical Research Council (M.R.C.) in Edinburgh. He recommended me to Professor Crofton and after my six month stint at Dublin, I proceeded to the City Hospital, Edinburgh. Tuberculosis was the global scourge at the time and in 1955, few countries world-wide could have undertaken the massive trials that were now taking place throughout the U.K.

Research into Tuberculosis, like in other diseases was laborious, pernickety and at times, plain boring. But for those who led us, a satisfying result was in the offing. Everything was very well organised. I could carry out ten lumbar punctures on tubercular meningitis' patients in the space of one hour. These tests and treatments were carried out at weekly intervals. A sister accompanied me. At the foot of each bed, a trolley with all the necessary instruments required for the puncture and other tests awaited. A nurse stood by the trolley. If there were eight patients—there were eight trolleys. Everything worked and worked well. The matron and sister were still in full command. The wards were divided into male and female. All had their blood, urine and sputum tested weekly. Depending on which day of the week you were admitted, would determine your length of hospital stay and outcome. The patients of each ward were treated with one of the many combinations of anti-tubercular drugs. If you were lucky, you improved quickly, for the best combination of drugs, for a successful outcome, was in your ward. When I first arrived in Edinburgh, there were long waiting lists for hospital admission. By the time I left, six months later, there were none. The wards were emptying at a rapid rate. The scourge of the century was now on its way to eradication. Most of the specialists, unless they could diversify, would in the short run become self-redundant. With their experience and new knowledge, few would have done so for long, for the diseases of the chest were now on their way to being recognised as a speciality in their own right. The free time available, was similar to Dudley, except that after 5pm little inpatient work came my way. Occasionally cover for a visit to the cinema could be arranged. My travels to Dublin via Larne-Stranraer continued, irrespective of the weather-conditions. Snow and ice between Edinburgh and Larne, and storm conditions in the Irish Sea were not a bar to this ardent lover!

My Edinburgh experience showed clearly how an organised hospital functions, when medical research is at its zenith. But whilst chest x-rays, were moving into a diagnostic tool, other pulmonary shadows were making their way in. Patients entering hospital, for their very long stay, were divided into 2 groups: those that smoked more than a packet of 20 cigarettes a day, and those who smoked less or none. The association between lung cancer and smoking had been made, a year or two earlier, at Oxford. Now, Edinburgh was joining the investigations.

In 1955, during my summer holidays in Gibraltar, I passed the best anti-tubercular combination that I had learnt from the M.R.C. trials to Dr Giraldi. I knew from that date, if used, that the tuberculosis problem for Gibraltar was over and that the K.G.V. Hospital as a sanatorium, could be confidently expected to close, within a very short time. Tuberculosis was on its way out from 1955, as the trials showed.

From Edinburgh I moved to Dundee, where I undertook a locum for a very large general practice, whilst its principal was caravanning in Italy. I soon learnt how general practice should not be run.

West of England Eye Infirmary. Exeter

Whilst in Dundee, I applied for an ophthalmic post in Exeter at the West of England Eye Infirmary. I did not expect to get the appointment. Unfortunately following the interview, I was accepted. The costs involved for my interview; train, food etc could not be re-imbursed, until I returned to take up my appointment some weeks later. With less than £1 in my pocket and a long journey ahead to Edinburgh, to meet my father, I now had a major travelling problem. From Exeter to London was easy: a penny platform ticket sufficed with a signed note to the ticket collector that I would pay within a month. I ate some sandwiches on the train. The long walk from Paddington to Euston station was not difficult. I now had 2 pence in my pocket and I needed one more to ring Gerald Marco, who would have solved my financial problem. I ended up begging for one penny, which produced a negative public response. My only chance now was to seek help from the police. "We have a doctor here, who has no money, and wants his father's help to pay his rail ticket to Edinburgh." Whilst it became a police joke for 20 minutes, the Edinburgh police voice sobered them up. My father was the main guest speaker at a major Edinburgh public event. Politeness now reigned; a night sleeper was arranged and £10 to see me through. It was the first and last occasion I sought financial help from him, following graduation, for I intended to be financially self sufficient from that date on. Young doctors in the UK were exploited to the maximum by their NHS conditions of employment.

The world of ophthalmology was now open to me at Exeter's West of England Eye Infirmary. There were three consultants and one clinical assistant and the clinics were always full. The medical and surgical parts of eye diseases was very interesting, but what was not, was refraction. "Refraction is and will be your bread and butter". I was not convinced. What did finally convince me was the abnormally high rate of hypostatic pneumonia that occurred following cataract extraction. All the patients were old and were all told to stay still following the operation. By the time my contract ended, I was well-versed in ophthalmology's common ailments. Six months prior to this appointment, I had proposed to May, and she had accepted.

Royal Alexander Hospital, Rhyl

From Exeter, I moved to the Royal Alexander Hospital in Rhyl, North Wales. My new appointment was as casualty officer. From my Vespa's point of view, Rhyl was a stone's throw to Holyhead, manageable in a few easy hours. My casualty work was not difficult and the going easy by Dudley standards. Halfway through my contract, I crossed the Irish Sea once more, this time to marry May, in Limerick.

The Wedding and the Honeymoon

Two weeks maximum leave was all that my contract allowed. Not that that mattered, for my salary was so low that I could not financially afford a longer honeymoon. Fortunately Willie and others gave cheques for wedding gifts, and this helped considerably to pay for our honeymoon and some months later, our return to Gibraltar.

The day before the wedding I crossed the Irish Sea. In keeping with Irish tradition, I could not see my future wife, for 24 hours before the ceremony if luck was to be on the newly weds' side. By the time I arrived in Limerick, all my Irish friends and guests were already there. I was the last one. Unfortunately none had brought their invitations with them and as a result, no-one including the groom, knew the name of the church where the wedding was to take place. We knew the time but not the place. We woke early the next day, in the hope that we would locate the correct one, for Limerick is a city full of spires and churches. One church, no. Two, no, now time was running short. At the third church, I saw one of our guests, O'Gorman Quinn, who had been a pupil of Stonyhurst in my father's time. He and his wife were standing outside the church's entrance. My panic subsided. We had managed to arrive on time, but only just, for 20 minutes later, as tradition demands, the beautiful bride arrived. Her two pretty sisters Rita and Alice were her bridesmaids. The wedding went off to perfection for we had four priests and one senior Christian Brother (May's uncle) attending at the sanctuary. After the wedding ceremony, our reception was held at Bunratty Castle. It was a sumptuous sit-down banquet, as only the Irish could do so well.

Other than those of my sister and Aunt Mema, the number of weddings I had attended, was small as a result of war and my absence from home. When it came to the bridegroom's speech I became tongue-tied, for I had no idea what my address should be all about, even though, weeks before I had sought advice. However I did manage to say two words: 'Thank you' before I sat down. Those that followed me were so eloquent with their speeches that they must have kissed the Blarney Stone.

Jimmie Milliken, my good friend at Trinity had lent me his brand new Morris Minor, for our journey across Ireland; from Limerick to Dublin. We would be flying from Collinston to Heathrow Airport by Ireland's national airline Aer Lingus. The distance from Bunratty to Collinston was about 140 miles. The cars, new or old, always gave trouble and usually when you least expected it. Yet this time the Minor never gave us trouble and we arrived on time for our London departure.

The Tavistock Hotel in Tavistock Square was our home from home, for two nights. To the right of the hotel was located the headquarters of the British Medical Association. The next night we saw the musical 'Hernando's Hideaway', which we thoroughly enjoyed. Next morning we bussed to Heathrow for Gibraltar, refuelling at Barajas, Madrid. There was now no need to refuel in Bordeaux, for the fuel tanks in the new planes could fly the extra distance. Progress!

Our second reception was to be held in Secretary's Lane, for my family considered, that few Gibraltarians would attend the Limerick wedding, due to the travelling difficulties that most would have experienced getting there. My father had met May some years before in Dublin (S.4), and the rest of my close family had been corresponding with her. We began with tea and drinks at home, to meet all my family and then on to the Rock Hotel. A large bouquet of red roses adorned our hotel room with a note from my brother Willie, congratulating us. The manager, Emilio Manet, generously presented us with a bottle of champagne and a free 48 hour stay at the hotel.

The next day, brought the big reception at Secretary's Lane where several hundred guests were in attendance. My poor wife had to meet them all: not only the guests, friends, but my extended family as well. She performed superbly well and was an instant success, as expected.

Before we left for the second stage of our honeymoon, which was to include Seville, Madrid, Granada and Torremolinos, my father, during lunch advised us as to where to go, including museums, sites worthy of seeing, good restaurants etc. They would make our honeymoon memorable. With the good advice came the warnings: no night travelling from city to city for fear of bandidos; refill your fuel tank prior to leaving the city, for there are very few petrol stations on the highway and above all, respect the grey uniform policemen. They are 'Rottweilers' and will take you into custody, if you disagree. Obey them. Don't argue.

Spain in 1956 was still in poverty mode, with the begging hand visible everywhere. Food was cheap and their beer enjoyable. The devastation of the Civil War was visible all round and in many areas had not been tackled, even though 20 years had elapsed. The Guardia Civil and the 'Rottweilers' were everywhere. The result was a crime free country. Children in tattered clothing stared hungrily as they wandered about city streets.

Willie had lent me his Opel car for our honeymoon. It journeyed well. At Madrid suddenly and without apparent cause, the gear box ceased. There were no spare parts available. Spanish motor mechanics were the best in the world for if given time, they could make the necessary part, if you waited.

Prior to returning to Gibraltar, we decided that we needed a good tan. We stopped at Los Nidos (The Nests) in Torremolinos, which lay a few metres from the beach. Unfortunately, our next door neighbour had 'the runs' that night. His toilet must have been separated from our bedroom by the thinnest wall possible, for we were kept awake until 4am. An hour earlier, I had knocked at his door and given him my anti-diarrhoea mixture, which I carried, just in case. It worked and all of us slept soundly thereafter.

Next day was Sunday, so we drove to Malaga Cathedral for mass. We were stopped by the 'Rottweilers', a kilometre from our place of worship. They demanded to see our passports, which we did not have with us. It was mandatory for foreign nationals to hand in their passports to the hotel receptionist. So this we had done. An argument now ensued between my wife and the 'Rottweilers', in which I became the interpreter. We lost but only because we were in Spain. "You must always carry your passport when travelling: mass or no mass. That is the law". On our return from the hotel, half an hour later, and with our passports in hand, we found the 'Rottweilers' had left. We were late for mass.

So our honeymoon ended and it was back to the Royal Alexandra Hospital and casualty. We now lived in a flat 300metres from the hospital. Spring came early that year, and with the good weather came the holidaymakers. Whilst my hospital work prior to marriage was easy and relaxing, it was quite another matter on our return. The 'summer season' had begun and with it came the vacationers by the hundreds and in ever increasing numbers as we approached July. My workload multiplied four-fold and as it increased virtually on a daily basis, my married life moved to a standstill. This was not on. I had not married May for her to be my cook and caretaker. I resigned my job giving a month's notice and brought my mother-in-law to Rhyl for a two week holiday.

Following my resignation, we left for Kilkee, a small seaside town on the west coast of Ireland, known for its wild and natural beauty, and rain, when you least expected it. It was to be our farewell to Ireland and its good inhabitants who had made my years there, extremely happy. From now on, I would return on a yearly basis, but only during the summer. I left Ireland in very happy mode, for I left it with one highly prized possession: May, my Irish wife.

Chapter 10

THE RINGROSE

My wife's family name is Ringrose. They were a distinguished military family that settled in County Clare, Ireland. In 1556, Richard Rose, an Englishman from Hampshire, England, was ceremoniously awarded a gold ring by Queen Elizabeth, as a reward for his distinguished military service and bravery in the Queen's Army. As a result of such an honour, he proposed to the Queen a change to his name, which was to include the word 'ring': from Rose to Ringrose. His request was granted at Queen Elizabeth's command. They were a military family; Protestant and in the 17th century, English settlers in Ireland.

The first was Colonel Richard Ringrose. He came with Cromwell's model army, in response to the Irish Rebellion of 1641. Within 10 years, Cromwell had defeated the Irish Catholics and royalists. The re-conquest of Ireland was marked by large scale 'plantations' notably in Ulster and Munster; the dispossession of Irish landowners who had rebelled against the Crown, and the granting of their land to the colonists; in the south, to the English and in the north, to the Scots. The terms of the plantation, particularly in Ulster, were very harsh on the native Irish population, who were forbidden from owning, renting or working on lands in plantation areas. Cromwell, as the result of his brutality and contempt for his enemies, was often referred to as 'the butcher'. The Ringroses loyally served the English Crown, Cromwell and the Kings and Queens of Great Britain, with distinction. As English military settlers, they were granted land in County Clare, and their family home near Scariff was 'Moynoe House.' At varying times and for 200 years, they held the high positions of High Sheriff; Justice of the Peace; Colonel and others.

From Protestant to Catholic

Thomas Ringrose (B. 1822), raised as a Protestant, was my wife's great grandfather. He married Margaret Ryan, a Catholic. She was nearly half his age. It is thought that she agreed to the union provided any children born would be raised in her faith. She spent the rest of her married life with Thomas, in a virtual continuous state of childbirth: 11 in all. Thomas' ownership of Boulnacausk, their home, proved to be a brief one, as his father's death, preceded his own by less than 10 months. In 1857, under Irish Law, a marriage ceremony for a couple, one spouse of which was Protestant and the other Catholic, carried out in a Catholic Church was invalid for the Protestant. By the year of Thomas' death in 1879, the estate was damaged beyond repair. To a large part this was due to his conversion from the privileged state of a 'settled' to one of the settled. The start of Parnell's Land War left the embattled

Protestant class with no inclination to aid an estate, now presided over entirely by Catholics. 'In early Edwardian times, Margaret and her children left Meelick Co. Clare. All family association with its Protestant ascendancy background now came to an end. The religious denomination of Thomas' children was also significant in relation to their education. The Catholic education was more expensive. None of Thomas' children died from the potato famine, as a result of their privilege settler position. The Potato Famine of 1845-49, devastated an impoverished Ireland decimating its Catholic poor by hundreds of thousands. About 1 million were believed to have died.

THE RINGROSES AND OTHERS. S.

Stonyhurst Philosophers
(1908).

STONYHURST PHILOSOPHERS, 1908.
MESSRS. J. VILLAS BOAS, J. SAKATES, J. DE WOELMONT, M. TIESENBACHER, C. COULSTON.
MESSRS. J. KAVANAGH, D. RYAN, C. RYAN, A. DE LILHERVELDE, R. DE BEAUGIANIES, G. FITZ, H. WHIZELL, O. STOLBERG, A. COOKE
MESSRS. F. DE LA TORRE, A. ASCHAN, A. LIDDELL, B. SMITH, J. PLUNKETT, J. JOSIKA, J. OF TROOSTEMBERCH.
MESSRS. K. CALLAGHAN, J. EYRE, E. TROUP, F. WALDROFF.

Eight years later, Aidan Liddell was awarded the VC and then died of wounds and Joseph Plunkett was executed for his part in the Easter Rising in Dublin. **1**

Michael in uniform with Bridget Ringrose.

May (2nd left) and family Kingston *(1934).*

S.

Father meets May for the first time and is "delighted".
Dun Laoghaire.

May, sisters and mother. Kilkee; Co Clare.

My wife *(1956)*.

May with Brian. Kilkee, Ireland. *(August 1957)*.

S.

May and Cecil with the Ringroses at Bunratty Castle, County Clare. *(3 April 1956).*

May and Cecil at Bunratty Castle.

Eamon De Valera *(1960).*

Evening Herald. *"Happy Couple".*

S.

Rita and Alice (sisters) with the happy couple.

"I got her". Au revoir, Ireland.

Capt Billy Ringrose of the Irish Equestrian Team receiving the Grand Prix Cup from H.M. Queen Elizabeth II in Rome. *(1961)*.

Australia

After 1822, emigration to Australia was more attractive to would-be Irish emigrants than to America, for the sea-passage was mainly aid-provided. Pre-1822, convict transportation from Co. Clare was insignificant amounting to only 82 people, nine of whom were women. Between 1821-40, 636 Clare people were transported to New South Wales, Australia, principally for petty crime—stealing bread; butter; clothing; killing sheep for meat all done in the name of survival. More serious crimes, including the stealing of cattle, earned life sentences to Australia. These 'convicts' sent home word about the superior kind of life available in the colony. In the 1820's a number of 'free' settlers, with capital, relocated there. Most of them came from the landed gentry, merchants, professionals and the educated classes. Others who were free of crime and were residents of the poor houses; the unemployed; the unemployable (due to the harsh penal laws), and poor people, who were unable to survive on their small plots of land also migrated. The latter were 'exported' since it was cheaper to pay for their sea-passage than to maintain them in Co. Clare. As there was a preponderance of male immigrants, the governors of the Australian states, requested greater female numbers. To this end, the Co. Clare. Board of Guardians offered free passage to orphan girl inmates, aged between 14 to 18 years. Such a request had a dual purpose. It lessened the financial burden of the orphans' (and others) upkeep, paid for by their Clare Guardians, and helped the Australian Governors, with an indigenous, 'Born by Birth', population. Of Thomas Ringrose's 11 children; 2 died in infancy; 1 emigrated to the United States and enlisted and 3 emigrated to Australia; 2 boys (Richard B.1860),

(Thomas B.1863) and 1 girl (Bridget B.1875). John (B.1858) fortunately remained in Ireland. He was my wife's grandfather.

'Anzacs'

May's great-uncle, Thomas who had migrated to Australia in 1891, returned with the 'Anzacs' and fought on the ill-fated Gallipoli Beaches, where he was wounded. (He gave his age as 44). After he recovered, he was sent to the Battle of Fromelles 'where in the initial assault, the Anzac Battalion suffered casualties to 65% of its fighting strength' and then in 1916 to 'The Battle of the Somme'. He survived. He was temporarily medically discharged and returned to see his mother in the family house at Meelick, Co. Clare. Whilst there, he was interrogated during a night-time raid by the police and British Army.

His nephew Thomas (B.1895) was involved in the 1916 Rising and partook of republican activities. Despite serving in the Australian Army, which was itself under the ultimate command of the British Army, Thomas (B.1863) appeared to believe that Irish soldiers serving in the British army were misguided.' Richard (B.1860) Thomas' brother serving with the Anzacs, was also at Gallipoli, but as the result of war wounds to his eye, was medically discharged from the army. His 3 nephews Thomas, Jack and my wife's father Michael (S.2) went on to play an important part in the formation of the Irish Republic, as it is to-day.

Michael was the youngest son of John Ringrose (B.1858). Born a Roman Catholic he married Brigid Malone (S 2), the world's best mother-in-law: no ifs or buts. Her second child, May, I was to marry. None of the eight children now born to John emigrated, which was unusual at the time. None of the sons joined the British Army in the Great War of 1914, for their generation belonged to the '1916 Irish Easter Rising'.

In 1914, Thomas joined 'the Irish Volunteers', the armed militia established by the Irish Nationalists, to ensure the British implemented the Home-Rule Act, which granted self-government. In 1914, the Irish Nationalist Party held every parliamentary seat in Ireland other than in the Unionist strongholds of Dublin and Ulster. Willie Redmond, the East Clare Nationalist M.P. at Westminster, held this post from 1900 until he was killed at the battle of Messines in 1917. His famous quotation in 1914 during a recruiting speech in Cork: "I do not say to you, go—but grey haired and old as I am, I say come, come with me to the war". He was 53 and was commissioned a major. The vast majority of the Irish Volunteers joined the 16th Irish Division of the British Army. There was no conscription in Ireland, as the voluntary rate was nearly equal to the conscripted rate in England or Scotland. 'Conscription would have been vehemently opposed, by all shades of nationalist opinion.'

Following Redmond's death, Eamon De Valera (S 10), a U.S. citizen, stood as a candidate for the Sinn Féin party. 'He had been nominated while still in a British jail, for his role in the 1916 Rising'. He had not been summarily executed, as he held a U.S. passport. 'His manifesto called for complete separation from Britain and if necessary with force, and non-recognition of the British Parliament'. He was elected for East Clare (including Meelick). De Valera had the open support of the Catholic Church.

In 1919, the Irish Volunteers were renamed the Irish Republican Army. The three brothers, Thomas, Jack and Michael were early recruits. Prior to the Easter Rising of 1916, a Modus Vivendi existed between Britain and Ireland, but only just. Once the 'Easter Rising' was ruthlessly quashed, the Irish mood toward Britain radically changed. Those partaking in the Dublin Easter Rising, including the wounded, were summarily executed and without trial. Amongst them was Joseph Plunkett. In the Stonyhurst Philosophers' photograph of 1908 (S 1), which was reprinted in the Stonyhurst Association's Newsletter of 2008, the following was recorded under the class photo. 'Eight years later, Aidan Liddell was awarded the V.C. and then died of wounds and Joseph Plunkett was executed for his part in the Easter Rising in Dublin.' Plunkett was the son of papal count George Noble Plunkett who was the curator of the National Museum. He was a Nationalist, a poet, and a leader of the 1916 Easter Rising. Anger throughout Ireland was the result of the summary executions. Britain was fully involved in the Great War at that time.

The British solution to tame the Irish were the 'Black and Tans'. This much-hated paramilitary force was largely recruited from decommissioned military and other more thuggish men. Their aim was to counter the 'illegal' paramilitary force now growing throughout Ireland: the Irish Volunteers. In modern times, the 'Black and Tans' would have been considered a state terrorist organisation. They acted as one. At Dublin's Croke park, they machine-gunned a crowd of innocent and unarmed bystanders. In East Clare, they set on fire large numbers of houses with one purpose in mind: to terrorise the Irish into submission. In the winter of 1920, all able-bodied men present in Scariff, Co. Clare were lined up, their shirts removed and publicily horse-whipped. Few had a good word for the 'Black and Tans' and much less for all their actions.

During the Anglo-Irish War of Independence (from Britain) 'the Republican Army was under the overall command of General Michael Collins'. He was a revolutionary leader and M.P. for Cork South in the first Dail of 1919. He was a member of the Irish delegation during the Anglo-Irish treaty negotiations. He was Minister for Finance and Director of Intelligence. He was charismatically known as the 'Big Fella'.

Michael Ringrose (S 2), my wife's father, was 'active' during the 1919-22 Civil War. He had joined the Republican Army and in 1922 was transferred to the Irish Free State Army (the new name) and still under the command of General Michael Collins. It is said that he was the youngest officer in the Irish Army. He was forced to resign his commission with many others, following the mutiny of 1924. The mutineers outlined their demands, amongst them, the removal of the Army Council; an end to demobilisation, from 55,000 at the end of the Civil War to 15,000, and that the Government should do more to create an 'All Ireland Republic' of 32 counties! Aware of Mussolini's Blackshirts and his 1922 Coup d'état, the Irish Free State cabinet demanded the resignation of the entire Army Council. The generals resigned as did many junior officers (including Michael) associated with them, affirming, the subservience of the military to the now civilian government. In 1922, General Michael Collins was tricked, ambushed and killed by a posse of his enemies.

Michael's brother, Thomas continued with his military career until his retirement. Two of his sons followed; Billy attaining a colonel status and his brother Desmond a captaincy. The latter resigned his commission for greener pastures.

Some years before meeting May, I had met Captain Michael Turbidy, with his wife to be, Dot Lawlor (P 17 front row) through Deirdre Mulcahy (P 17—sitting 2nd left), a very good friend of Felim Meade who I knew at Stonyhurst. Within a very short time, Michael had won three equestrian Grand Prix; two in Dublin and one in New York. He tragically died in a riding accident. Michael, like Billy Ringrose and his brother Desmond belonged to the Army Equitation School. All were exceptional world class show jumpers.

At the time of writing, Colonel Ringrose is not only the Chef d'Equipe of the Irish team, but is currently the President of the Royal Dublin Society (R.D.S).

In his earlier years, Billy won the New York and Harrisburg Grand Prix. But it was in 1961 when the Elizabethan full circle finally closed on the Ringroses. At the 'Equestrian Grand Prix' held that year in Rome, (S 14 - 17), Billy won the world's most prestigious show-jumping cup. Queen Elizabeth II presented him with the prize: from English to Irish; from Protestant to Catholic; from Settler to Settled and from Ring to Cup. It took nearly 400 years to complete the Elizabethan circle. And I am the lucky recipient to marry May: a Ringrose.